MASTERS OF MUSIC

BACH

AND BAROQUE MUSIC

TEXT
STEFANO CATUCCI

ILLUSTRATIONS
STUDIO BONI-PIERI-CRITONE, *with the contribution of*
SERGIO, GIAMPAOLO FALESCHINI, AND MANUELA CAPPON

63469

BARRON'S

DoGi

HOW TO READ THIS BOOK

English translation ©
Copyright 1998
by Barron's Educational
Series, Inc.
Original edition © 1997
by DoGi srl Florence Italy
Title of original edition:
Bach e la Musica Barocca
Italian edition by:
Stefano Catucci
Illustrations by:
Studio Boni-Pieri-Critone,
Giampaolo Faleschini,
Sergio, Manuela Cappon
Graphic Display:
Francesco Lo Bello
Art Director and
page make up:
Sebastiano Ranchetti
Iconographic researcher:
Katherine Carson Forden
Editorial staff:
Andrea Bachini
Renzo Rossi
English translation by:
Venetia Scalo

Library of Congress
Catalog Card No. 98-72303

International Standard
Book No. 0-7641-5130-4

Printed in Italy

Each double page constitutes a chapter regarding the life and musical art of Bach, the great feats of the musical culture of his time (the Baroque Age) or the detailed analysis of the instruments and/or musical theory. The additional text to the left (1) and *the large central illustration refer to the principal theme. The text in italics (2) narrates the life of Bach in chronological order. The other elements on the page—photographs, printed reproductions of the era, portraits— complete the treatment of the discussion.*

ACKNOWLEDGMENTS

ABBREVIATIONS: h, high; b, below; c, center; r, right; and l, left.

ILLUSTRATIONS: The illustrations contained in this volume, unedited and original, have been obtained under the auspices and care of DoGi s.r.l., who holds the copyright.

CREDIT: Studio Boni-Pieri-Critone and Carlo Ferrantini, Lucia Mattioli, Armando Ponzecchi (4–5, 6–7, 12–13, 14–15, 20–21, 22–23, 26–27, 28–29, 30–31, 32–33, 38–39, 40–41, 46–47, 52–53, 54–55); Manuela Cappon (16–17, 48 below left); Luca Cascioli (10 center); Lorenzo Cecchi (44–45); Giampaolo Faleschini (8–9, 10–11, 34–35, 56–57); L.R. Galante (42); Francesco LoBello (48–49); Andrea Ricciardi (18–19, 24–25); Claudia Saraceni (33 high right, 36–37, 41 high right, 50–51); Sergio (58–59, 60–61)

TITLE PAGE: Studio Boni-Pieri-Critone
COVER: Studio Boni-Pieri-Critone
LIST OF REPRODUCTIONS:
DoGi s.r.l. has made every effort to trace all third-party rights. We apologize for any omissions or errors and will be happy to make any corrections in all future editions of this work.

We express our thanks to Barbara Steinwachs at the BACH-ARCHIV LEIPZIG for her collaboration.

The works that have been reproduced in their totality are followed by the letter **t**; those that have been reproduced in part are followed by the letter **p**. **6hl** Albrecht Dürer, *Martyrdom of the Ten Thousand,* 1508, plate transferred to canvas, 38 × 34 in (99 × 87 cm) (KUNSTHISTORISCHES MUSEUM, VIENNA) p; **6hr** F. Puget, *Reunion of Musicians,* painting, end of the seventeenth century (LOUVRE, PARIS) p; **7** Carl Röhling, *Bach plays for the royals in the music room of the Sans-Souci Palace,* 1890, wood engraving (AKG, BERLIN) p; **8cl** Carl Seffner, *Monument to Bach in Leipzig,* lower portion of the Thomaskirche, sculpture, 1908 (AKG/Dieter E. Hoppe, Berlin) t; **8bl** *Bach's Genealogical Tree* (BACHHAUS, EISENACH) t; **9** Johann David Herlicius (signed), *Johann Ambrosius Bach, Court Announcer and Trumpeter in Eisenach,* a painting of the time, oil on canvas, 35 × 30 in (92 × 78 cm) (DEUTSCHE STAATSBIBLIOTECK, BERLIN) t; **10** Lucas Cranach the Elder, *Luther,* 1526, oil on wood (NATIONAL MUSEUM, STOCKHOLM) p; **11hr** Frontispiece of the Lutheran Bible (AKG, BERLIN) t; **11br** Bernard Picart, *The Communion of*

Lutherans in a Church of Augusta, 1732, engraving (BIBLIOTHEQUE DES ARTS DECORATIFS, PARIS) p; **12** Thomas Hudson, *Georg Friedrich Händel,* painting (STAATSBIBLIOTECK, HAMBURG) p; **13** Anonymous, *Domenico Scarlatti* (Igda, MILAN) p; **14** Anonymous, *Presumed Portrait of Claudio Monteverdi,* painting of the seventeenth century (Rcs-Igda, MILAN) p; **16hl** Johannes Voorhout, *Allegory of the Friendship of Buxtehude (with Score) and Johann Adam Reincken (at the harpsichord),* 1674, oil on canvas, 48 × 74 in (125 × 190 cm) (MUSEUM FÜR HAMBURGISCHE GESCHICHTE, HAMBURG; AKG, BERLIN) p; **16hr** Matthäus Merian, *Landscape of the City of Lübeck,* copper engraving, printed in color by Topography Saxoniae Inferioris (AKG, BERLIN) t; **17** Johann Ernst Rensch, *Johann Sebastian Bach,* circa 1715, painting (ANGERMUSEUM, ERFURT; AKG BERLIN) p; **18** Anonymous, *Organ of the Church of Saint Eustache in Paris,* watercolor, 1801 (JEAN LOUP CHARMET, PARIS) t; **20** Christian Fritzsch, *Erdmann Neumeister,* engraving (BACHHAUS, EISENACH) p; **21** Bernard Vögel, *Christiane Eberhardine, Princess of Saxony,* lithograph (AKG, BERLIN) p; **22** Valentin de Boulogne, *Concerto for Six People,* seventeenth century (LOUVRE, PARIS; ARCHIVIO ALINARI/GIRAUDON/ LAUROS, FLORENCE) p; **23l** J.S. Bach *The Art of the Fugue,* page 17 of the manuscript of the score (SMPK, STAATSBIBLIOTECK; AKG BERLIN) t; **23r** Anonymous, *Giovanni Pierluigi di Palestrina,* circa 1567 (MUSEO DEL CONSERVATORIO, NAPLES) p; **24hl** Anonymous, *Arcangelo Corelli* (Igda, MILANO) p; **24hr** Anonymous, *Presumed Portrait of Antonio Vivaldi,* oil painting (CIVICO MUSEO BIBLIOGRAFICO MUSICALE, BOLOGNA) p; **26hl** Anonymous, *Louis XIV Interprets the Sun King,* color print, 1651 (MARY EVANS PICTURE LIBRARY, LONDON) t; **26bl** Anonymous, *Jean-Baptiste Lully,* sixteenth-century engraving (PALACE MUSEUM, VERSAILLES) t; **27bl** Anonymous, *Presumed Portrait of François Couperin the Great,* circa 1695 (PRIVATE COLLECTION) p; **27br** Hyacinthe Rigaud, *Louis XIV* (LOUVRE, PARIS) p; **28hl** Anonymous, *Giuseppe Tartini* (CIVICO MUSEO BIBLIOGRAFICO, BOLOGNA) p; **28hr** Attributed by Julius Schloffer to A. Ciciliano, *Cello* (KUNSTHISTORISCHES MUSEUM-NEUE BURG, VIENNA) p; **29hc** Matteo Stella, *Anterior and Posterior View of the Small Theorbo Constructed in Venice,* 1638 (MUSEE INSTRUMENTAL DU CONSERVATOIRE NATIONAL

SUPÉRIEUR DE MUSIQUE, PARIS) t; **29hr** Hamman, *Stradivari,* engraving (GIUNTI EDITORE, FLORENCE) p; **31** Anonymous, *Cristian Ludwig,* oil painting (AKG, BERLIN) p; **32hl** William Hogarth, *Inn for The Beggar's Opera,* 1728 (RAINSVILLE ARCHIVE, LONDON) p; **32bl** William Aikman, *John Gay,* oil painting (SCOTTISH PORTRAIT GALLERY, EDINBURGH) p; **34hl** Anonymous, *George II* (ARCHIVIO DOGI, FLORENCE) p; **34bl** Denis Diderot and Jean-Baptiste Le Rond d'Alembert, *Encyclopedia,* volume I, frontispiece (AKG, BERLIN) p; **35bc** Anonymous, *Fireworks on the Thames at Whitehall on May 15, 1749 in the Presence of the King* (VICTORIA AND ALBERT MUSEUM, LONDON) t; **35cr** Anonymous, *Philipp Telemann,* engraving (AKG, BERLIN) p; **36** Anonymous, *King's Theatre in Haymarket,* watercolor (THE BRITISH MUSEUM, LONDON) p; **37hr** William Hogarth, *Farinelli with Cuzzoni and the Little Sienese,* engraving (MUSEO TEATRALE ALLA SCALA, MILAN) p; **37br** Jacopo Amigoni, *Farinelli,* detail of a portrait with his friends Teresa Castellini and Pietro Metastasio, circa 1751 (Igda, MILAN) p; **38hl** Jean-Baptiste Lully, *Theseus,* score, 1711, Paris (CINQUE SECOLI DI STAMPA MUSICALE IN EUROPA, ELECTA NAPLES) p; **40** *Facade of the Church of Santa Maria di Vallicella* (PAOLO SORIANI, ROME) t; **42hl** Andrea della Robbia, *Saint Matthew Evangelist,* 1491, ceramic (SANTA MARIA DELLE CARCERI, PRATO; ARCHIVIO ALINARI/ARCHIVIO SEAE, FLORENCE) t; **42hr** Andrea della Robbia, *Saint John Evangelist,* 1491, ceramic (SANTA MARIA DELLE CARCERI, PRATO; ARCHIVIO ALINARI/ARCHIVIO SEAE, FLORENCE) t; **43** (1–6) Giotto, *Scenes from the Life of Christ,* 1302–1306, frescoes (CAPPELLA DEGLI SCROVEGNI, PADUA) t; **44hl** Johann Gottfried Krügner, *Thomaskirche at Leipzig,* 1723, color copper engraving (AKG, BERLIN) t; **44bl** E.G. Haussmann, *Portrait of Johann Matthias Gesner, Rector of the School of Saint Thomas,* oil on canvas, eighteenth century (PRIVATE COLLECTION) p; **44c** Anonymous, *Interior of St. Thomas Church,* engraving (BACH-ARCHIV, LEIPZIG) p; **46hl** Johann Jakob Ihle, *Portrait of Johann Sebastian Bach,* painting, 1720, oil on canvas, copy of the original, 26 × 32 in (82 × 66 cm) (BACHHAUS, EISENACH; AKG BERLIN) t; **46b** Benjamin Hill, *Pocket Watch,* circa 1750 (ARCHIVIO DOGI, FLORENCE) t; **47hc** Anna Magdalena Bach, Frontispiece of *Notenbüchlein,* 1725 (AKG, BERLIN) t; **47hr** Balthasar Denner (attributed), *Bach and His*

Three Sons, detail of the portrait of Wilhelm Friedemann, painting, 1730 (PRIVATE COLLECTION) p; **48hl** Gustav Schüler, *Harpsichord Concerto,* copper engraving, 1794 (AKG, BERLIN) t; **49hr** Frontispiece of *The Goldberg Variations* of J.S. Bach; **50hl** Georg Emanuel Opitz, *Claßigs Caffeehaus,* Leipzig, 1820, color lithograph (AKG, BERLIN) t; **50b** Anonymous, *Open-air Concerto Given by a Group of Students at Leipzig,* engraving (BACH-ARCHIV, LEIPZIG) p; **51hr** Johann Georg Schreiber, *Caffé Zimmermann,* engraving (MUSEEN DER STADT, LEIPZIG) t; **52** Anonymous, *Frederick II of Prussia,* oil painting (STAATLICHE MUSEEN, BERLIN) p; **54** Manuscript of the score of the *Musical Offering* of J.S. Bach, 1747 (DEUTSCHE STAATSBIBLIOTECK; AKG, BERLIN) t; **55hr** Anonymous, *Portrait of Baron Gottfried van Swieten,* engraving (MUSEEN DER STADT, VIENNA) t; **55br** Barbara Krafft, *Portrait of Wolfgang A. Mozart after His Death,* 1814, painting (ERIC LESSING, VIENNA) p; **56h** Coat of Arms of J.S. Bach (AKG, BERLIN) p; **57hr** Jacques-André-Joseph Aved, *Jean-Philippe Rameau,* oil on canvas (MUSÉE DES BEAUX-ARTS, DIJON) p; **58hl** Anonymous, *Portrait of Wilhelm Friedemann Bach* (Igda, MILAN) p; **58hr** Anonymous, *Portrait of Johann Christoph Friedrich Bach* (Igda, MILAN) p; **58b** Anonymous, *Mozart at Six Years Old,* 1763 (INTERNATIONALE STIFTUNG MOZARTEUM, SALZBURG) p; **59hr** Heinrich Pfenninger, *Portrait of Carl Philipp Emanuel Bach,* engraving (HAYDN MUSEUM, VIENNA) p; **60h** Signature of J.S. Bach (AKG, BERLIN) p; **60b** J.S. Bach, *Manuscript Page for Anna Magdalena,* 1725 (AKG, BERLIN) p; **61h** Anonymous, *Portrait of Johann Nikolaus Forkel,* (Igda, MILAN) p; **61b** Anonymous, *Cello Player,* England, seventeenth century (EXPLORER, PARIS) t.

CONTENTS

THE PROTAGONISTS

Johann Sebastian Bach lived in an age of changes that, within a sixty-five-year period (1685–1750), profoundly transformed the sensibility of European man: it was the Baroque Age and music was at its center. Vivaldi and Corelli invented the language of the modern orchestra, Händel and Rameau that of the melodrama, Buxtehude and Scarlatti elaborated upon a virtuosity rich in expression, while artisans such as Stradivari and Silbermann developed new Baroque musical instruments. Musical battles were fought between singers and intellectuals, and the impulses of princes and patrons encouraged the birth of a light and gallant style. In the face of so much variety, there was only one experience that could not be tampered with in the Baroque Age: the search for beauty.

♦ **ANTONIO VIVALDI AND ARCANGELO CORELLI**
The two recognized masters of the Italian style: their music transformed the language of the Baroque orchestra and influenced an entire epoch.

♦ **JEAN-PHILIPPE RAMEAU**
The supreme French musician of the 1700s was also a theorist and one of the founders of modern harmonic theory.

♦ **DIETRICH BUXTEHUDE**
He worked as an organist in Lübeck. When Bach was still a boy, Buxtehude was the most important musician in all of Germany.

♦ **ANTONIO STRADIVARI AND GOTTFRIED SILBERMANN**
A legendary Italian lute-maker and a great German organ-maker: they are responsible, in part, for developing the musical instruments of the Baroque Age.

♦ **DOMENICO SCARLATTI**
He was an extraordinary virtuoso on the keyboard of the harpsichord: his music, whimsical and sometimes frenzied, was the Baroque emblem.

♦ **SENESINO (THE LITTLE SIENESE) AND CUZZONI**
A castrati (eunuch) and a capricious soprano: they were the most famous singers of Italian opera, quintessential prima donnas paid very high wages, especially by English theaters.

♦ **FREDERICK II**
King of Prussia, absolute sovereign, but enlightened. He played the flute, wrote poetry, loved art and the artists with whom he surrounded himself. It was from one of his ideas that Bach's *The Musical Offering* was born.

♦ **GEORG FRIEDRICH HÄNDEL**
Together with Bach, he was the major musician of the Baroque Age. Famous throughout Europe, he moved to England, where he worked predominantly on melodrama.

♦ **PRINCE LEOPOLD OF ANHALT-CÖTHEN**
Bach was employed in his service from 1717 to 1723: the happiness of his creative phase during this period depended in large measure on the largesse of the musical visions of this prince.

♦ **WILLIAM HOGARTH**
An English painter who was not afraid of venturing into the realm of social criticism; in London, he shared in the success of popular theater with his drawings.

♦ **JOHN GAY AND JONATHAN SWIFT**
A poet and a novelist: two intellectuals of great influence who in England waged a battle against the conventions of Italian opera in favor of a theater concerned with the present, which would not exclude political satire.

♦ **ANDREAS WERCKMEISTER**
He was the theorist of the "compromise," indeed, of a tuning system that resolved many problems of intonation and rendered more efficient rules of harmony.

JOHANN SEBASTIAN AND ANNA MAGDALENA BACH
Bach's work, not always understood by his contemporaries, celebrated the values of faith and reason. Upon his death, his wife remained impoverished.

♦ **THE MARGRAVE OF BRANDENBURG**
He was one of the most powerful princes of Germany. *The Brandenburg Concertos* are dedicated to him.

♦ **CARL PHILIPP EMANUEL AND JOHANN CHRISTIAN BACH**
Bach's older sons: excellent musicians, their fame eclipsed their father's throughout the 1700s.

GERMANY

Toward the end of the 1600s, Germany was still feeling the effects of the bloody war that had lasted for thirty years (1618–1648). The population had been reduced by half, manual labor was scarce, famines, epidemics, a reduction of all economic activities, and extreme fragmentation of territory and power all occurred. Slowly, however, the desire to live and to travel blossomed. The German princes tried to increase their prestige by promoting the arts and culture. Thus, the Golden Age of the German Baroque was born: exuberant architecture began to change the face of the cities, while refined and ambitious music helped solidify the community.

♦ THE THIRTY YEARS' WAR
From 1618 to 1648 Germany was torn apart by a war between Catholic and Protestant princes. The long and bloody war had involved the armies and civilian populations of the major powers of Europe. The peace agreement, signed in Westphalia in 1648, had divided Germany into more than 300 principalities of various sizes, each with legislative and religious autonomy. There were eight principalities that had the right to vote in the election of the Emperor, but after the war three regions had become stronger: Bavaria, Brandenburg, and Saxony. There also existed 66 minor principalities governed by Catholic hierarchies and another 203 lay principalities, and 53 small local sovereignties. Fifty-one autonomous cities and about 1500 urban centers were granted the right to enforce laws and administrative regulations. Above is a detail of Dürer's *Martyrdom of the Ten Thousand.*

♦ MUSICAL INSTITUTIONS
Three institutions generally regulated the musical activities of cities: the cultured population, the court, and the municipal music groups. The autonomy of the various centers favored the growth of local schools and styles. Above, a detail of *Reunion of Musicians* by F. Puget.

♦ SALARIES
Those who covered public debts, such as musicians, received by contract an annual quota of wine, wheat, and wood to compensate for their low wages.

♦ ARTISANS
The German princes based their manufacture of porcelain on the French model, but for a long time the craftsmanship was limited to products that were strictly utilitarian.

◆ THE MARKET SQUARE
The market square was where the fabric of German society began to mend itself after the war. It was always near the municipal buildings: goods and money were scarce, but people went to the square to restore their ties to the community, to gain solidarity, and to welcome those who came from nearby cities.

◆ THE ARCHITECTURE
The German princes spent a great deal of money to beautify and decorate the cities: French elegance dominated, but the whimsicality of the Baroque style was stifled by the desire for geometry.

◆ THE MUSICAL PROFESSIONS
The position of cathedral organist was a stable one at the time and for this reason was very sought after, even if it was less well-paying than the job of choir master. At a slightly lower social grade was the position of the cantor, director of a musical school. Above, Bach in a detail of a lithograph.

◆ RELIGIOUS AUTHORITIES
In parts of Germany, the religion that prevailed had been reformed by Luther and had separated from the Church of Rome. Religious authorities influenced public life and promoted, through their teachings, the unity of the German language, the foundation of a spreading nationalistic sentiment despite the fragmentation of the territory.

THE LIFE OF BACH

1. ◆ *Johann Sebastian Bach was born on March 21, 1685 in Eisenach, a city of Thuringia with a population of about 6,000, to a family of very old and far-reaching musical traditions. It was his father, Johann Ambrosius, director of the city's musical service, who taught his son the rudiments of the art. At nine years of age, within a few months, Johann Sebastian lost both his mother, Elizabeth, and his father. He was then entrusted to his brother, Johann Christoph, an organist in the nearby city of Ohrdruf. Here, singing in the school choir and studying the organ, Sebastian revealed his exceptional talent.* ⇒

THE MUSICIAN'S CRAFT

When Sebastian was born, music had been a part of the Bach family for more than one hundred years: his grandparents and many other relatives were musicians; some of his many children would become musicians. Bach's life story coincided with the transformation of the musician's craft from the 1500s to the 1700s: it followed the dilettantism in which playing a musical instrument was just a diversion and ultimately transformed into the epoch in which the composer was the glory of the national culture.

♦**JOHANN SEBASTIAN** (1685–1750)
Organist, musical director, and teacher in various courts and choirs. The most important member of the Bach family was above all a composer: his work became a lasting cultural legacy.

♦**THE MONUMENT**
Leipzig dedicated it to Sebastian in 1843: in the modern epoch, the musician became the glory of the nation.

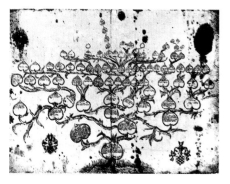
♦**THE GENEOLOGICAL TREE**
In 1735, at the age of fifty, Sebastian reconstructed the geneological tree of his own family, citing as many as 53 musicians in a time frame of less than two hundred years. The last musical descendant was Wilhelm Friedrich Ernst Bach, who died in 1845 and who was present at the dedication of the monument erected in honor of his great-uncle at Leipzig.

♦**JOHANN AMBROSIUS** (1649–1695)
Father of Sebastian. He played the violin and the trumpet, he directed the municipal band of Eisenach, and he wrote music for the town fanfare.

♦**HANS BACH** (1580–1626)
He was a baker like the father of Veit, but also a rugmaker and minstrel in his spare time. During the Thirty Years' War he fled from Gotha, his native city, and died in Wechmar of the plague in 1626.

♦**JOHANN JAKOB** (1682–1722)
Brother of Sebastian, he was an oboist in the army of King Charles XII of Sweden, with whom he was also able to study the flute. Following this, he became the court musician in Stockholm, the city in which he died.

♦**CHRISTOPH BACH** (1613–1661)
Grandfather of Sebastian, he was in the service of the Duke of Weimar as a domestic, gardener, and member of the court orchestra. He was the first Bach who was able to make a living from his activities as an instrumentalist.

♦**VEIT BACH**
Deceased about 1577, legend has it that he was the first Bach musician. He was a baker. He possessed a small zither (lyre) that he brought with him to the mill and that he tried to play in time to the rhythm of the grinding.

♦**BACHS BEFORE SEBASTIAN**
"Johann" was almost a family name for the Bachs, all of whom at home and in public had the custom of calling themselves by their last names. And if Sebastian settled the family's geneological tree, his father Ambrosius (pictured above) had in his time gathered the works of his ancestors, organizing them in a kind of anthology destined for his children and grandchildren who wished to perfect their studies. This collection, known as *Alt-Bachisches Archiv (Old Bach Archives),* was subsequently completed by Sebastian and later by one of his sons, Carl Philipp Emanuel, the same person to whom was entrusted the conservation of the geneological tree. It consists, in all, of twenty compositions of various types, with a prevalence of sacred cantatas that testify to the profound religious tradition of the family.

RELIGION

♦ **MARTIN LUTHER**
(1483–1546)
He was the promoter of the Reform that in the mid-1500s divided Christian Europe in two. His was above all a battle, a protest (hence, Protestantism) against the doctrine and the corruption of the Roman Church: the only norms of faith that Luther recognized were those contained in the sacred scriptures, not those imposed by the pope and bishops. To enable even the less educated a way to read the sacred texts for themselves, Luther translated the scriptures into German. Moreover, he revised the rite of the Mass, rendering it more open to the participation of the faithful through the practice of choral singing. But the Reformation was also a battle of power: the German princes supported Luther to free themselves from the interference of the Roman church and to defend themselves against the popular revolts in Germany that were gaining momentum in the name of the new religion.

The Thirty Years' War was the final episode of a religious conflict that began in 1517, when the German monk Martin Luther set forth an objection to the Catholic Church of Rome, a proclamation destined to divide in two the Christian population of Central Europe. Luther's Reformation brought the Protestant Church to life, based on the reduction of the power of priests and on a more direct participation of the faithful in the religious experience. Luther translated the Bible into German to render it accessible even to those who did not know Latin and attributed an important role to music, considering song to be a "prayer said twice." All of Bach's sacred work manifests a profound adherence to the Lutheran faith.

♦ **BAPTISM**
For the Catholic Church, this was the sacrament that purified the newborn from Original Sin. For Luther it was the manner in which the community welcomed a new Christian and sent him on the road of the faith.

♦ **GERMANY**
When Bach was born, the German states of the North (in pink), richer and more densely populated, had for some time embraced the reformed religion. When the religious conflicts were over, the fragmentation of Germany became stabilized on the basis of reciprocal agreements of tolerance.

2. THE LIFE OF BACH ♦ *Sebastian remained in his brother's home for four years, during which time he contributed to the family's finances with money he earned singing in the choir. In 1700 he left Ohrdruf and moved to Lüneburg to follow more advanced courses of study. This city was larger and wealthier than those in which he had lived up to that time, and it was close to Hamburg, the crossroad for cultural influences coming from all of Europe. Bach, who spent a great deal of time listening to music, assimilated the diversity of musical styles, concentrating on both sacred and theatrical music.* ≫♦

♦ **THE BOOK OF SONGS**
In 1524 Luther published the first edition of the *Book of Spiritual Songs,* the basis of the entire tradition of the Protestant choir.

♦ THE CHOIR
The basis of Protestantism's sacred music followed the model indicated by Luther. It favored the participation of all the faithful: simple melodies, strict rhythm, texts that express an elementary faith.

♦ THE SERMON
In the Lutheran Church, priests had the task of commenting on the readings in the form of a sermon before and after which the musicians performed the cantata.

♦ THE MASS IN B MINOR
Luther had conserved the use of the Latin language for the principal parts of the Mass, limiting the use of German to the texts, sacred songs, and other Bible readings. This division generally reflected a type of music that was modern and simple in style in the German language; it had a more severe type of music for the Latin parts. Bach succeeded in synthesizing these two tendencies in a single work with his grandiose *Mass in B Minor,* a monumental work in Latin. The definitive edition reappeared during the last years of Bach's life, but in reality, it was just recycled material written over the course of a much longer period of time. Above, the title page of Bach's Bible; below, an engraving of the Communion rite of Lutherans.

♦ COMMUNION
Luther was opposed to the almost superstitious significance that Communion had assumed in the Catholic Mass, but did recognize its profound symbolic value and believed it to be useful in reinforcing the faith.

♦ SCHOOL
The Lutheran Church supported an elementary-level instruction that adhered to and spread the practice of reading the sacred scriptures. The Latin schools, which prepared students for university studies, were therefore the more popular German schools.

THE BAROQUE AGE

Baroque was the language of exuberance, of imagination overcoming discipline, of the decoration that brought surfaces to life and that lightened structures. In music, however, more than a precise style, the Baroque represented a mixture of diverse styles. Dance and theater, virtuosity and lyricism invaded every area and assimilated in a single language even the characteristics of local schools. Two protagonists emerged: Händel and Scarlatti. They were born in the same year as Bach, but they never met him. However, Händel and Scarlatti met in their youth, and in Rome they competed in a famous contest of skill on the harpsichord and organ, which reflected the Baroque taste and pomp.

♦ HÄNDEL
The life of Georg Friedrich Händel (1685–1759) paralleled that of Bach, who represented the opposite and complementary musical pole. He was born in Halle, a few kilometers from Eisenach, where Bach was born. His family did not have a musical tradition. His father, who had been a barber and became the surgeon of the Duke of Saxony, wanted his son to study law, not music, but Händel secretly practiced at the keyboard, in the attic, until he obtained permission to combine his legal studies with those of music. At the age of twenty-one, he departed for Italy, where he quickly became famous for his operas. At twenty-seven years of age, he settled in London, England, where he remained for the rest of his life, gratified by a success never before achieved by any artist. He produced music that was whimsical, brilliant, suitable for the theater, but effective in the religious sphere as well.

♦ ARCANGELO CORELLI
Virtuoso violinist and composer, he was the guest of Cardinal Ottoboni in Rome.

♦ CARDINAL PAMPHILI
He was one of the first to finance Händel in Italy, who wrote some cantata lyrics for him.

♦ HÄNDEL
By the admission of Scarlatti himself, Händel won the organ competition.

♦ PIETRO OTTOBONI
A cardinal in the church, he organized weekly concerts at the Chancery. He was the one who initiated the contest between Händel and Scarlatti, both of whom were his protégés.

♦ SCARLATTI
At the harpsichord, he was equal to and perhaps superior to his adversary.

♦ CONTESTS OF VIRTUOSITY
Typical of the Baroque style:
in the theater these contests
occurred between singers; in
private palaces, between players
of individual instruments.

♦ THE PALACE OF THE CHANCERY
It was the residence of Cardinal Ottoboni in Rome. The contest between Händel and Scarlatti took place here, in the first months of 1709.

♦ TRAVEL REPORTS
Travel reports, such as those of the French scholar Charles de Brosses (1709–1777), brought news of the musical life of other nations. Imprecise, but important in the formation of a public opinion, accounts of voyages spread throughout Europe, as did reports of the contest between Händel and Scarlatti.

♦ FRANCESCO MARIA RUSPOLI
Marquis, great music connoisseur, protected Händel, who was Protestant, from the pressures of the Roman Church.

♦ SCARLATTI
Almost all of the work of Domenico Scarlatti (1685–1757) is dedicated to the harpsichord, an instrument that he played with unparalleled virtuosity and for which he wrote more than 500 sonatas. He debuted as an opera writer in Italy and England, but abandoned the melodrama at the moment in which, in 1729, he transferred to Lisbon in the service of Maria Barbara of Braganza, whom he also followed to Madrid upon her marriage to the heir to the Spanish throne, the future Ferdinand VI. Isolated from the rest of the musical world, Scarlatti cultivated a style far removed from the popular styles. His technique was exceptional: rapid arpeggios, crossed hands, hammered notes. What interested him most in the sonatas was the novelty of an idea, an unexpected harmony, an extravagant passage which he repeated like an obsession, thereby hastening new inventions.

3. THE LIFE OF BACH ♦ *At Lüneburg Bach was far from his native region, Thuringia, but not from the sphere of influence of his extended family. Following his first appointment as a violinist at Weimar, in 1703 he was called by an uncle to give an organ concert at Arnstadt, a small town with less than 4000 inhabitants, in his own Thuringia. The pretext was a test of the recently restored instrument: Sebastian, at eighteen years of age, astounded the audience and secured the position of organist.* ➥♦

THE MYTH OF ORPHEUS

During the Baroque Age, music became the language of feeling par excellence. Its goal was to move the public, to express sentiment. The true protagonist of the epoch was the song itself, a simple melody accompanied by one or more instruments. Musical theater flourished, and authors looked to classical mythology for stories that integrated sounds and dramatic representation. The myth of Orpheus imposed itself, and for more than two centuries remained the musical symbol that the strength of sentiment could defeat even death. Monteverdi's *Orfeo (Orpheus)*, staged in Mantua in 1607, became the model of the entire Baroque musical theater.

♦ MONTEVERDI
After having revived polyphony with his *Otto Libri di Madrigali,* Claudio Monteverdi (pictured above, 1567–1643) gave form with his *Orfeo* to the genre of the melodrama, indeed, to the union of theatrical action and music, that up to that time had lived as an experiment with a different result. A few years prior, in Florence, Jacopo Peri and Giulio Caccini were inspired by Orpheus to produce controversial works with polyphony conducting, a technique in which the sung parts tended to have a spoken tone of recitation. The melodies were richer, but the instruments and the treatment of voices in a group assumed a new expression. The expression of sentiment was evident, and produced an adequate resonant representation.

♦ THE MYTH
Orpheus descends to the realm of the dead, and by the beauty of his song, he is able to bring back among the living his beloved Eurydice, provided he does not gaze at her during his return. But Orpheus turns toward her and Eurydice is lost.

♦ THE ORCHESTRA
For *Orfeo,* Monteverdi prepared an orchestra of unusual dimensions with respect to the past: he not only gave depth to the choruses, to the arias, to the dances, but also to the development of the expressive capacity of the music.

♦ THE MUSIC
Typical of the Baroque style was the prologue, in which the ideas that bore out the opera became embodied in one character as in an allegory: in Monteverdi's *Orfeo,* the music dominated.

♦ ORPHEUS
Son of the muse Calliope and husband of the nymph Eurydice; Apollo gave him the gift of a lyre with which he could enchant, with divine harmonies, animals, savages, and trees, and awaken rocks and inanimate objects.

♦ CHARON
In his boat, he brings souls to the realm of the dead. To allow Orpheus to pass, the god Apollo puts him to sleep.

♦ PERSEPHONE
A divinity of Hades, the realm of the dead. She intercedes with Pluto for the salvation of Eurydice.

♦ PLUTO
Divinity of the realm of the dead. He consents to Orpheus's desire to enter the domain of the inhabitants of hell to bring his beloved Eurydice back to life, on the condition that Orpheus not turn to look at her before leaving the underworld. But Orpheus is unable to do this. Hearing noises behind him, he turns and loses Eurydice forever.

♦ APOLLO AND VENUS
Venus is the goddess of beauty; Apollo is the patron of the arts: they are the ones who protect and guide Orpheus.

♦ EURYDICE
She was always interpreted as a soprano voice. The part of Orpheus was rendered as a masculine or feminine voice: in Monteverdi he was a tenor, in Gluck, author of the more famous *Orfeo ed Euridice (Orpheus and Euridice)* of the 1700s, he was a contralto, a female voice of deeper timbre.

A MUSICAL PILGRIMAGE

✦ **BUXTEHUDE**
The work of Dietrich Buxtehude (1637–1707) was fundamental to the development of German sacred music in the 1700s. Of Danish origin, from 1668 he worked in Lübeck, in the Marienkirche, one of the most important organist posts in all of Germany. The legacy of the old masters of the Nordic schools resounding in his style is enriched by an instinct for grandiosity, a typical trait of Baroque art. He dedicated music of exceptional virtuosity to the organ: departing from the genres of Lutheran tradition, he constructed forms that were ever richer and which codified the mechanisms of the fugue, a type of composition often used by Bach. Buxtehude even arranged the modern form of the sacred cantata, alternating between choral and solo parts, enlarging the orchestra, and refining the operatic writing.

The division of German territory into numerous principalities and sovereignties resulted in differences, even in the development of the arts and culture. Travel therefore became a fundamental element in the formation of an artist. Moving from one city to another meant meeting prestigious masters, coming into contact with diverse schools and traditions, and breaking the routine of one's own position. Having obtained permission from his superiors, Bach traveled nearly 250 miles (400 km) on foot to go to Lübeck to meet the great Buxtehude in 1705.

✦ **LÜBECK**
City of ancient commercial and maritime traditions, Lübeck boasted a very old musical tradition, closely tied to Marienkirche, seat of a very important choir dating back to the Middle Ages.

✦ **TRAVEL**
By carriage, the distance between Arnstadt and Lübeck could be covered in three days of travel, with two horse changes a day. For Bach, who could not afford to hire a carriage, the journey took nine days on foot.

4. THE LIFE OF BACH ✦ *In Arnstadt, Bach had many conflicts with the authorities and with his fellow students. One of these, Geyersbach, who had been admonished by Sebastian for the way he played the bassoon, lay in wait with other companions armed with clubs, for Bach one night. They attacked and Bach defended himself with a sword. The incident ended up in the tribunal. Shortly after, the city council admonished Bach for the excessive length of his stay in Lübeck and for the length of the music he wrote after his return, while still under Buxtehude's influence.* ≫✦

✦ **BACH**
He left Arnstadt with permission for a four-week leave to go to Lübeck and stayed four months. Upon returning, he was reprimanded.

♦ **EVENING MUSIC**
Evening music in Lübeck boasted long tradition and was organized by merchant guilds. Buxtehude made it famous throughout Germany for its very theatrical style and an excellent forty-piece orchestra.

♦ **THE ORGANIST'S CONTRACT**
The position of organist was dependent upon the civic authorities and was paid with public money. In Arnstadt, where musical activity was rather modest, Bach (above, in a youthful portrait) had a contract that gave him, in fact, a great deal of liberty. The salary was 30 thalers for room and board, withdrawn from the municipal hospital funds, plus another 50 florins, which came from church offerings and the local tax upon inns. In exchange, the organist had to play in church on Sunday mornings, from 8:00 A.M. to 10:00 A.M., on Monday afternoons for choral practices, on Thursday mornings from 7:00 A.M. to 9:00 A.M., and on all other days of worship. He was responsible for the proper care of the instrument and was expected to conduct himself in a manner that was beyond reproach. Another task was the preparation of the church music with choir members and instrumentalists.

♦ **SCHIEFFERDECKER**
Mediocre organist, he married Anna Margreta and thus inherited the position of his father-in-law, one of the more coveted musical positions in Germany.

♦ **ANNA MARGRETA**
Daughter of Buxtehude; her father's successor was expected to marry her. Bach, like Händel before him, refused her.

♦ **BUXTEHUDE**
His music "of the evening," full and rich with dramatic effects, was the model of Bach's cantatas.

How an organ is made

The organ is a fascinating and mysterious instrument; its sonorous power can fill a cathedral, the variety of its registers can imitate entire families of musical instruments, but the manner in which all of this is achieved remains hidden, screened behind the magnificent barrier of high silver pipes that often do not allow even the presence of the organist to be perceived. The "feeding system" of the air is out of sight, as is the wind chest where the air is collected and upon which the pipes rest. The most generalized articulation of the organ's parts or "elements" cannot be seen. The beautiful aspect and luxurious sound of organs were a reflection of the ambition of the Baroque courts, which invested substantial resources in them. The development of its delicate mechanisms has been the work of extraordinary artisans and of competent musicians, such as Bach.

1

2   3   4

♦ THE PIPES
The pipes have different shapes depending on their sound. There are flue pipes (2) and reed pipes (1, 4). The former are always open on top and make a sound resulting from the vibration of air produced around them from the opening that pierces their body. Their sound is similar to that of instruments such as the flute or the trumpet. The reed pipes are most often closed and, with various breaks, produce sound by means of the vibration of an internal membrane: they correspond to the registers of the oboe and the English horn. Made of wood and of various shapes are the staff pipes (3), the harmonic base of the musical phase.

♦ THE WIND CHEST
This is where the air accumulates and the pipes rest, arranged in rows according to their registers.

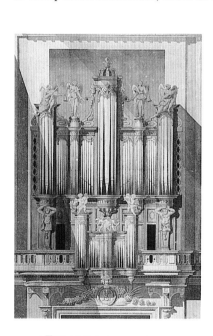

♦ THE FRONT OF THE ORGAN
A graduated front is required to combine functionality and appearance.

♦ THE BELLOWS
The resonance or sonority of the instrument depends on the bellows that produce air. For Bach, an organ always had to have "good lungs."

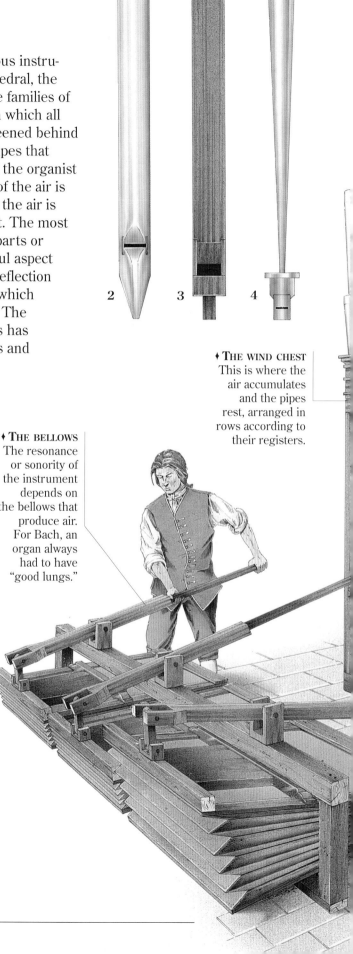

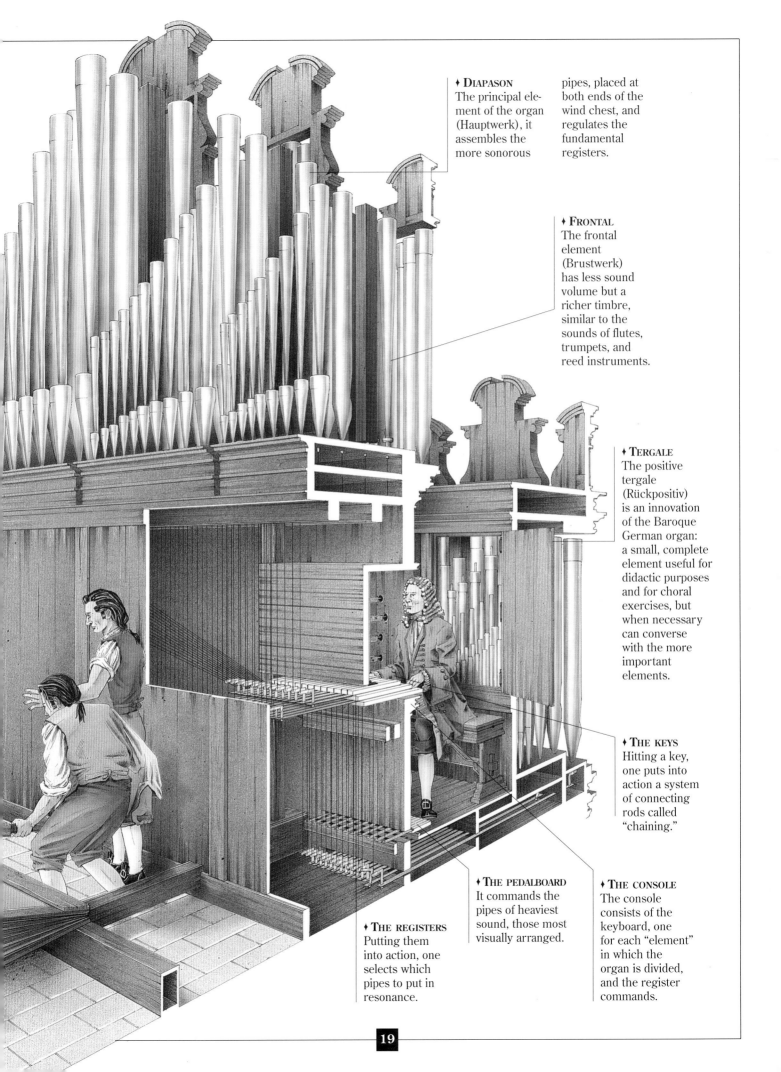

♦ **DIAPASON**
The principal element of the organ (Hauptwerk), it assembles the more sonorous pipes, placed at both ends of the wind chest, and regulates the fundamental registers.

♦ **FRONTAL**
The frontal element (Brustwerk) has less sound volume but a richer timbre, similar to the sounds of flutes, trumpets, and reed instruments.

♦ **TERGALE**
The positive tergale (Rückpositiv) is an innovation of the Baroque German organ: a small, complete element useful for didactic purposes and for choral exercises, but when necessary can converse with the more important elements.

♦ **THE KEYS**
Hitting a key, one puts into action a system of connecting rods called "chaining."

♦ **THE REGISTERS**
Putting them into action, one selects which pipes to put in resonance.

♦ **THE PEDALBOARD**
It commands the pipes of heaviest sound, those most visually arranged.

♦ **THE CONSOLE**
The console consists of the keyboard, one for each "element" in which the organ is divided, and the register commands.

THE CANTATAS

The cantatas, performed in church before and after the sermon, are the best testimony of the evolution of Bach's style: in a period of almost forty years, he gathered very different musical elements and organized them in a coherent form. The concertos and the operatic style of the parts entrusted to the soloists came from the Italian style. The use of dance rhythms came from the French style. But the heart of the cantata remained the syllabic melody of the Lutheran choir, with its mystic simplicity and the severe contrapuntal development to which Bach subjected it. Half of Bach's cantatas have been lost: in spite of this, we possess more than 200 sacred, and about 30 secular, cantatas.

♦ ERDMANN NEUMEISTER
(1671–1756)
He organized the cantatas, alternating chants and biblical verses with meditative verses.

♦ THE CONCERT INSTRUMENTS
An element of Italian derivation is the presence of concert instruments, with the function, that is, of soloists. Usually they conversed with voices during arias; less often they accompanied the entire cantata.

♦ BASSO OSTINATO
The execution of the harmonic base realized by the keyboard with other chosen instruments (cello, bassoon, and lute) improvising the bass notes.

♦ BACH
He began composing arias, then proceeded to choral music, and at the end he wrote recitatives.

♦ RECITATIVE
This is the harmonized recitation of a soloist that, usually accompanied only by the basso ostinato, links the episodes of the chorus and the arias.

♦ THE CHORUS

The chorus consists of four types of voices: two masculine—tenor and bass—and two feminine—soprano and contralto. In some compositions the chorus is doubled and divided in such a manner that one part alternates with the other in a play of reciprocal returns. Since it was forbidden for women to sing in church, the feminine parts were sung by "white" voices, that is, by children whose voices had not yet changed. Bach, who had a beautiful soprano timbre, sang in the choir until the age of sixteen.

♦ ONE OF BACH'S CANTATAS

This double page illustrates the structure of one of Bach's secular cantatas, the one catalogued with the initials BWV 198 and called *Trauerode*. The term "secular" indicates that the cantata had not been written for a holiday or festival, but rather for a special Mass: one in memory of Christiane Eberhardine, Duchess of Saxony (above), who remained faithful to the religion of Luther when her husband converted to Catholicism to receive the Crown of Poland. Performed at Leipzig on October 17, 1724, it is one of Bach's more ample cantatas. It is divided into two parts: the first opens with the chorus, continues with two arias with a recitative, and closes again with the chorus, always introduced by a recitative. The second part is shorter: an aria by the tenor, a recitative performed by the bass voice, and the final chorus. Being a secular cantata, the Lutheran choir, a crucial element in the sacred cantatas, is lacking.

♦ THE ORCHESTRA

Bach changed the structure of the orchestra according to style, expressive needs, and the forces at his disposal. Here we see one that is particularly ample: four soloist voices (soprano, contralto, tenor, and bass), a chorus of four voices, and violins, violas, cellos, bass violins, flutes, oboes, bassoons, horns, basses, lutes, and organ.

♦ THE ARIA

An elaborate composition for solo voices with musical accompaniment. The text expresses the feelings and thoughts of the character.

COUNTERPOINT

This term comes from the Latin *punctum contra punctum,* that is, "note against note": it is the art of superimposing two or more lines of melody that are called "voices," reminiscent of the epoch in which the counterpoint was the language par excellence of vocal music, of polyphony. The counterpoint proceeds from the starting point of a melody, imitating it in one or more different voices and developing each element according to rigorous geometric and mathematical proportions. The instrumental version of counterpoint is called the fugue. Bach was the greatest of its modern cultivators.

♦ THE FUGUE
The term "fugue" indicates an instrumental composition in which the counterpoint is widely used. Bach generally employed this model: A) exposition. The first voice intones a theme: the subject of the fugue. One after another, the other voices reproduce and imitate it, as in a game of reciprocal answers (ripostes). He followed with B) discussion. This is a series of musical episodes in which the material of the exposition, transported in a different tonality from the initial one, is reproduced in new imitations or else varied freely. Discussion was followed by C) stretto. This is the final phase of the fugue, often followed by a coda: there is a return to the original subject, and the game between subject and answer begins again: regarding the exposition, however, the voices intervene closer to each other. Above, detail of the painting *Concerto for Six People,* by Valentin de Boulogne, 17th century.

♦ SPECULAR
It is a canon form in which each note of a voice is rigorously symmetrical to the notes of the melody it imitates.

♦ VOICES
They are the single melodies that intertwine and insert themselves in the fugue.

♦ CANON
CANCRIZANS
The second voice takes the last note of the melody and proceeds backwards, like a claw.

22

◆ THE ART OF THE FUGUE
Bach so entitled his final work, the supreme synthesis of knowledge accumulated during his entire lifetime. Here, music comes close to the rigor of pure thought that is reflected through sounds.

◆ THE PLAY OF SOUNDS
The counterpoint is a method of combining sounds as if they were geometric figures, numbers, or images. Sprint, imitation, echo, recess, and reflection correspond to as many combination methods of the counterpoint.

◆ THE FLEMISH
In the 1400s, the Flemish elaborated the most complex forms of the counterpoint, developing in the most daring manner the techniques of imitation. Johannes Ockeghem (1428–1495) was the culmination of this ascetic and spiritual style.

◆ PALESTRINA
The work of Giovanni Pierluigi da Palestrina (1525–1594) was the beginning of a tradition of counterpoint that was different in many ways from that of the great schools of Northern Europe, primarily from the Flemish one. He had the same objections as the Roman Church, that deemed the language of the polyphony of the Protestants to be too artful and affected, and developed a more balanced type of construction. Palestrina's required that the words of the sacred texts be rendered comprehensible. Instead of putting at the forefront the mathematical calculation of the imitations, he tried to respect the declamation of the spoken word. In order to do this, Palestrina began with the melody closest to the tone of the prose, Gregorian chant, and elaborated on it in a counterpoint the very refined plot. On account of its dimensions and expressiveness, it can be defined as classical.

◆ THE CANON
A contrapuntal device whereby a single melody is repeated by different voices that enter in the distance in succession.

◆ IMITATION
One voice can imitate another not only by copying it to the letter, but also by modifying it with opportune rules of transformation.

◆ VARIATION
This is the procedure which transforms the basic melody, changing its form and shape.

THE ITALIAN STYLE

A new breeze animated music at the beginning of the 18th century: it was the Italian singable style, valued for its simplicity, its ability to express feeling and to convey images. It was about a language that was born in the theater and opera and which conserved the hierarchies that separate singers on the stage from the musicians in the orchestra. The concert, the typical form of this age, usually used solo instruments to interpret the principal part, leaving to the orchestra the role of accompaniment. The principles of this period spread throughout Europe. Even Bach studied them, transcribing some concertos of Antonio Vivaldi. The capital of this music was Venice, but other important centers were Rome and Naples. The principal composers were Vivaldi and Corelli, but behind them were excellent musicians such as Geminiani, Torelli, and Locatelli. All of them, prior to being composers, were excellent violin virtuosos, the primary instrument in the Baroque orchestra.

♦ CORELLI
Arcangelo Corelli (1653–1713) had linked his name to the grand concerto, the most important and widespread form of orchestral music of the first half of the 18th century. It is based on the dialogue of a variable group of solo instruments and the orchestra, called the "orchestral stuffing."

♦ VIVALDI
The Venetian Antonio Vivaldi (1678–1742) is the composer who has contributed most significantly to the affirmation of the Italian style. He wrote works for the theater, oratorios, motets, and other sacred pieces, but it was his concertos that brought him fame. His method of subdividing parts (three movements, alternating according to the sequence allegro-adagio-allegro) became canonic.

♦ CA' D'ORO
A very famous palace of Venetian Gothic style, it was built between 1424 and 1434. It gets its name from its polychromatic decorations, from its brilliant marbles, and above all from the gilt that once covered its facade.

5. THE LIFE OF BACH ♦ *In November of 1706 the authorities of the city of Arnstadt accused Bach of allowing a young foreign woman of making music with him in the choir, breaching the rule of male-only voices in church. Bach left the city, married the young woman—the cousin of Maria Barbara—and assumed the post of organist in the church of Saint Blaise at Mühlhausen. Arriving with great ideas, he soon clashed with the inertia of the local customs. Bach remained at Mühlhausen barely a year, just in time to be called to Weimar by the Prince of Saxony-Weimar.* ⇒

♦ CARNIVAL
The traditional festival of masks coincided, in Venice, with the season of music in the piazza, in aristocratic homes, and in conservatories where, in the 1600s, the best musicians played.

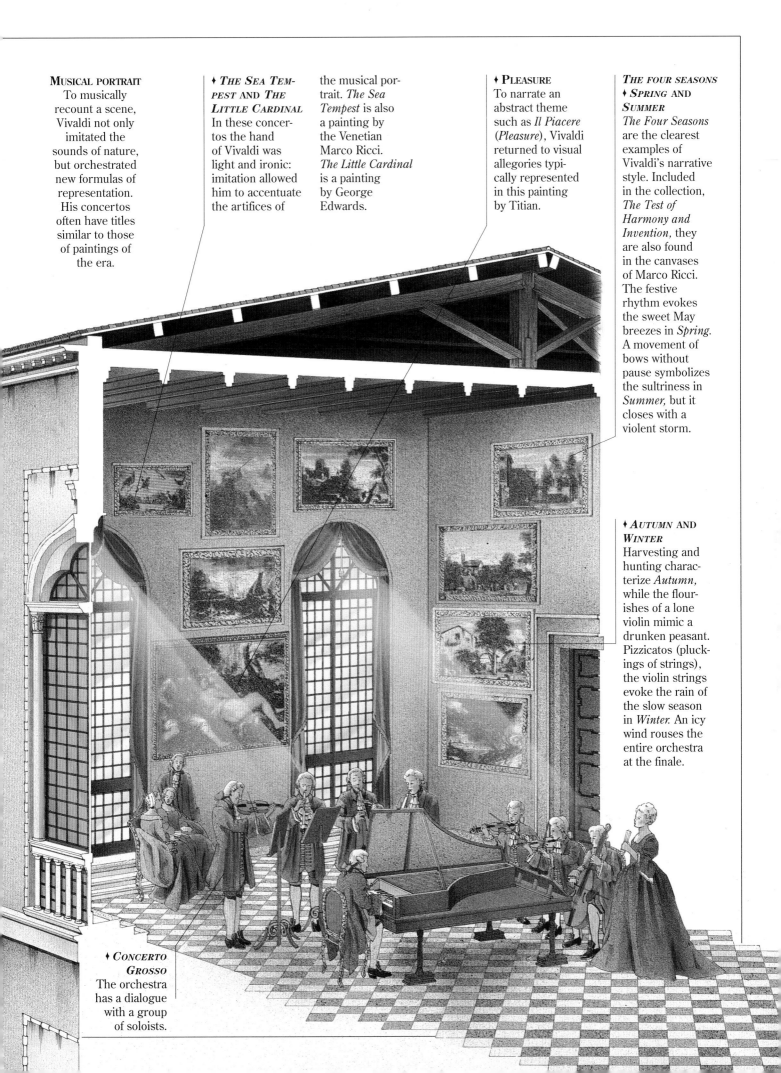

MUSICAL PORTRAIT
To musically recount a scene, Vivaldi not only imitated the sounds of nature, but orchestrated new formulas of representation. His concertos often have titles similar to those of paintings of the era.

♦ *THE SEA TEMPEST* AND *THE LITTLE CARDINAL*
In these concertos the hand of Vivaldi was light and ironic: imitation allowed him to accentuate the artifices of the musical portrait. *The Sea Tempest* is also a painting by the Venetian Marco Ricci. *The Little Cardinal* is a painting by George Edwards.

♦ **PLEASURE**
To narrate an abstract theme such as *Il Piacere* (*Pleasure*), Vivaldi returned to visual allegories typically represented in this painting by Titian.

THE FOUR SEASONS
♦ *SPRING* AND *SUMMER*
The Four Seasons are the clearest examples of Vivaldi's narrative style. Included in the collection, *The Test of Harmony and Invention,* they are also found in the canvases of Marco Ricci. The festive rhythm evokes the sweet May breezes in *Spring.* A movement of bows without pause symbolizes the sultriness in *Summer,* but it closes with a violent storm.

♦ *AUTUMN* AND *WINTER*
Harvesting and hunting characterize *Autumn,* while the flourishes of a lone violin mimic a drunken peasant. Pizzicatos (pluckings of strings), the violin strings evoke the rain of the slow season in *Winter.* An icy wind rouses the entire orchestra at the finale.

♦ *CONCERTO GROSSO*
The orchestra has a dialogue with a group of soloists.

THE FRENCH STYLE

To the bel canto of Italian derivation, France juxtaposed a music based on dance that blossomed under the reign of Louis XIV as an instrument of his absolute power. Musically educated, an excellent dancer, Louis XIV exhibited himself in court in pompous ballets that celebrated his reign with images taken from mythology. The role he preferred to dance was that of the god Apollo, whose cult is associated with the sun. But in his lengthy reign (1661–1715), the Sun King also concerned himself with the professional aspects of music: he established the first dance academy, he organized the largest orchestra of stringed instruments of the time, and he finally centralized all his musical power in the hands of a single artist, Lully, the true creator of the modern French style.

♦ LULLY
Florentine by birth, Jean-Baptiste Lully (1632–1687) arrived in Paris at the age of thirteen as the personal valet of the princess of Orleans. He studied violin, dance, and mimicry, and became a jester. At court, Louis XIV noticed him and made him his violinist. Lully (pictured below) composed many ballets and, with the playwright Molière, created the comedy-ballet. In 1672 he became the dominant figure in the musical life of France by assuming control of the production and staging of operas. His works, which evolved toward the genre of the lyric tragedy, enjoyed unprecedented success. In his last years, to accommodate the religious bent of his king, he dedicated himself to sacred music. Above, Louis XIV in one of the ballets of Lully.

♦ LOUIS XIV
He reigned from the death of Mazarino (1661) until 1715. He danced for the first time as Apollo in the Ballet of the *Feasts of Bacchus* in 1651. From then on he was often the protagonist in court ballets.

♦ GIULIO MAZARINO
Tutor of Louis XIV until 1661, he brought to France many Italian artists and instructed the king in the use of art to govern.

♦ ISAAC BENSERADE
(1613–1691)
A dramatist, he gave coherence to the court ballet; his flattering verses, with a mythological background, were particularly pleasing to the king.

♦ LULLY
In his lyric tragedies, he recaptured the diction that is typical of French theater actors and changed them into expressive and effective music.

♦ **DANCE**
At the beginning of his reign, Louis XIV founded the Royal Dance Academy and assigned a committee of nobles to renovate the technique.

♦ **THE SUITE**
Given its strong tie to dance, French instrumental music gave ample space to the genre of the suite, long considered an alternative to the Italian concerto form. The suite is precisely a series of very stylized dances of contrasting character: slow and fast movements, noble and peasant dances. In France, François Couperin (above, 1668–1733) wrote twenty-seven of them for the harpsichord and gave each one a descriptive title of typical Baroque taste, such as *The Majestic, The Proud, The Voluptuous.* Bach composed four of them in the French style for the orchestra (BWV 1066–69) and many for the harpsichord, introducing dances of English origin in each instance. Below, Louis XIV in a 1701 portrait.

♦ **MOLIÈRE**
(1622–1673) Jean-Baptiste Poquelin, known as Molière, was one of the greatest theatrical authors of all time. He collaborated with Lully, writing texts for court ballets in which dance numbers alternated with recited parts.

6. THE LIFE OF BACH ♦ *Weimar, the cradle of modern German culture, had at the time of Bach barely 5000 inhabitants. Sebastian remained there for almost nine years, from 1708 to 1717, as court musician. The musical ambience was lively, and for Bach it was a period of stability, disturbed only by his desire to become director of the court orchestra. Here Maria Barbara bore his first six children, two of whom—Wilhelm Friedemann and Carl Philipp Emanuel—would become excellent musicians.* ≫♦

INSTRUMENTS OF THE BAROQUE AGE

The Baroque Age witnessed a great development of lute-making, especially in the area of stringed instruments: violins of all types, held in the arms or supported by the legs, cellos large and small, violas and basses, but above all violins, skillfully constructed by great French and Italian artisans, the most celebrated of whom is Antonio Stradivari. During this time, musicians collaborated with artisans such as Tartini, who with his experience guided the work of the lute-makers. But the violins of the Baroque Age were different from those of today: less powerful and brilliant, sweeter and more tender.

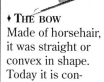

✦ GIUSEPPE TARTINI
He recounted about having heard performed by the devil, in a dream, a trill and some passages of extreme virtuosity, which he quickly reproduced in the sonata aptly called *Devil's Trill Sonata*. But Tartini (1692–1770) was also an avid student of acoustic phenomena. He made important discoveries on the effects of resonance, and he applied his knowledge to the techniques of lute-making, studying the relationship of the dimensions of the individual parts.

✦ VIOLA DA GAMBA
In the violin family, it was the typical Baroque instrument. It usually had six strings. It rested between the legs and had a very deep voice.

✦ THE THICKNESS OF THE WOOD
The lute-maker had to understand the exact measurement for each individual part: the quality of the sound depended on the thickness of the wood.

✦ STRADIVARI
The mixture of his varnishes was inimitable: his gold and red reflections were one of his secrets, together with the choice and thickness of the wood.

✦ THE BOW
Made of horsehair, it was straight or convex in shape. Today it is concave and produces a longer and more potent sound, but one that is less tender.

✦ THE STRINGS
They were made of intestines. For the larger instruments (such as the bass and the cello) they were covered in silver or copper. Steel strings are used today.

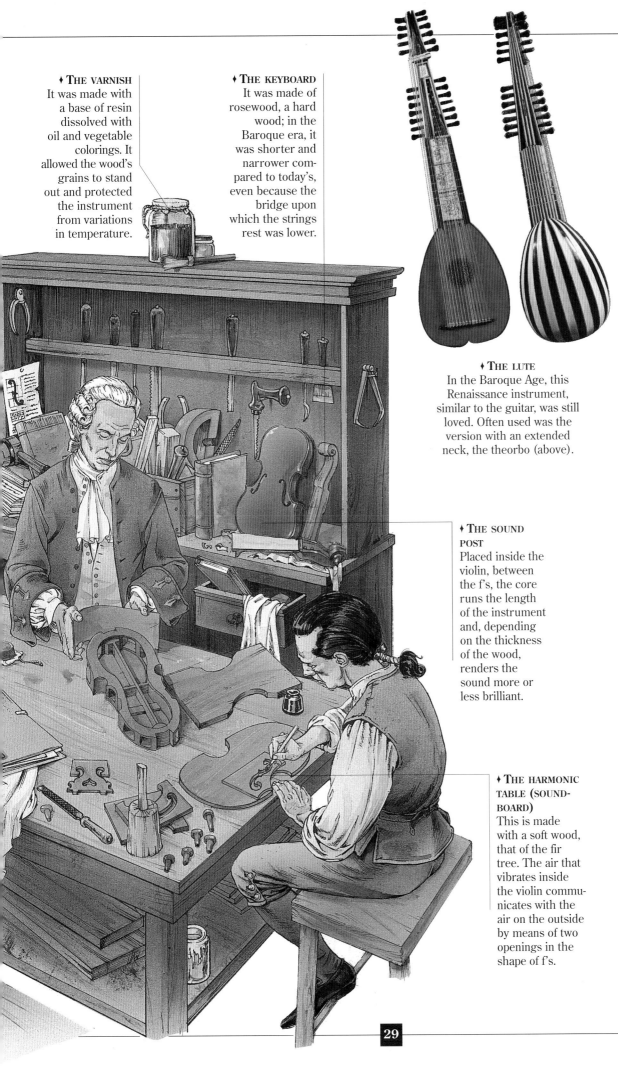

♦ THE VARNISH
It was made with a base of resin dissolved with oil and vegetable colorings. It allowed the wood's grains to stand out and protected the instrument from variations in temperature.

♦ THE KEYBOARD
It was made of rosewood, a hard wood; in the Baroque era, it was shorter and narrower compared to today's, even because the bridge upon which the strings rest was lower.

♦ THE LUTE
In the Baroque Age, this Renaissance instrument, similar to the guitar, was still loved. Often used was the version with an extended neck, the theorbo (above).

♦ THE SOUND POST
Placed inside the violin, between the f's, the core runs the length of the instrument and, depending on the thickness of the wood, renders the sound more or less brilliant.

♦ THE HARMONIC TABLE (SOUND-BOARD)
This is made with a soft wood, that of the fir tree. The air that vibrates inside the violin communicates with the air on the outside by means of two openings in the shape of f's.

♦ ANTONIO STRADIVARI
(c.1644–1737)
He was the greatest lute-maker of all time and the most celebrated representative of the school of Cremona (the true center of European lute-making during the entire Baroque Age), with the Amati, Guarneri, and Guadagnini families. As an adolescent, Stradavari worked in the shop of Nicola Amati. At the age of twenty-one he went out on his own and began the legendary production not only of violins, but also of violas and basses. His varnishes were so beautiful and remarkable that it was said he slept with his violins in production to transmit the warmth of his body to them. In reality, Stradivari's secret was all in the choice and preparation of the wood, upon which he spread a mixture of his own invention that rendered the porousness uniform. His instruments are still used to this day and are auctioned at exorbitant prices.

THE BRANDENBURG CONCERTOS

In 1724 Bach offered Christian Ludwig, Margrave of Brandenburg, six concertos that summarized the entire instrumental civilization of the Baroque Age. French and Italian keys alternated with each other, as did the modern techniques of the grand concerto and the archaic ones of the counterpoint. The variety of these concertos was due, in part, to the fact that Bach had collected materials accumulated over the course of fifteen years of work. The unity of the resulting work surpassed all musical limits of his time.

♦ **THE ORCHESTRA**
It is represented here in structure and arrangement, a Baroque orchestra, like the one that Bach put together at Köhten. For the performance of the *Brandenburg Concertos* only a few instruments were necessary, different for each concerto.

NO. 6 IN B-FLAT MAJOR
The oldest concerto in the collection has an archaic sonority. It is for strings alone, but it is the violas (IV) that express the major part of the melodic material.

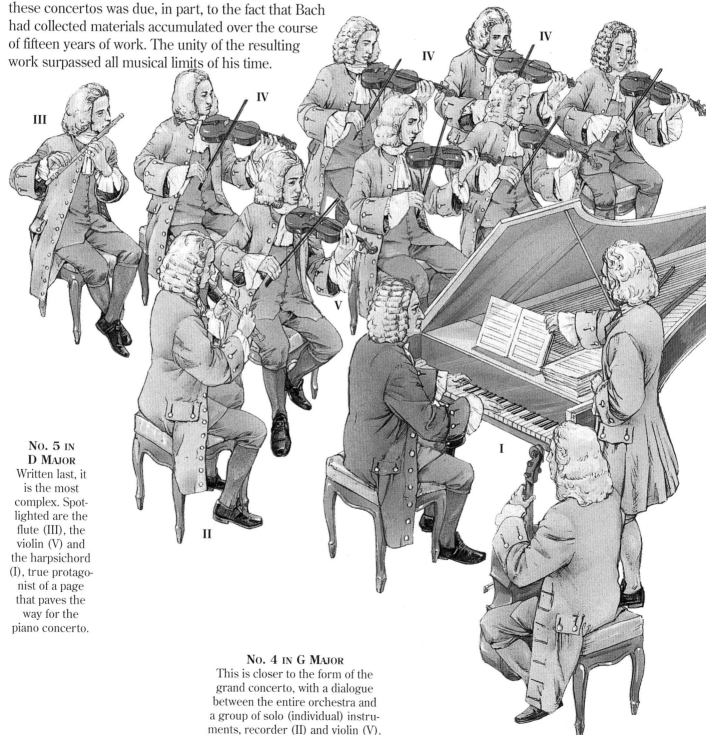

NO. 5 IN D MAJOR
Written last, it is the most complex. Spotlighted are the flute (III), the violin (V) and the harpsichord (I), true protagonist of a page that paves the way for the piano concerto.

NO. 4 IN G MAJOR
This is closer to the form of the grand concerto, with a dialogue between the entire orchestra and a group of solo (individual) instruments, recorder (II) and violin (V).

NO. 1 IN F MAJOR
The only one with four movements: it is in the French style and is therefore dominated by dance rhythms. The hunting-horns (VII) and the piccolo violin (VI) were very fashionable in France at the time.

NO. 2 IN F MAJOR
In the Italian style, it is airy and brilliant: a piccolo trumpet (VIII), very shrill, the recorder (II), and the oboe (IX) emerge. Of the three movements, the central one is the most meditative.

♦ THE MARGRAVE
Having received the six concertos, Christian Ludwig (at left) never had them performed. They were rediscovered in the 1800s by Friedrich Spitta, Bach's first biographer, who gave them the title by which they are known today.

NO. 3 IN G MAJOR
Like the sixth concerto, it is only for stringed instruments, without solo (individual) instruments, a compact and animated sonorous mass.

MUSICAL LIFE IN ENGLAND

♦ **THE BEGGAR'S OPERA**
Set in London's criminal under-world, it debuted in 1728, at Lincoln's Inn Fields Theatre. The text by the poet John Gay was violently satirical and attacked both the politics of the day—the minister Walpole in partic-ular—and the capricious whims of the prima don-nas of the Italian opera. The music was an assem-blage of popular songs and arias from famous operas arranged by John Christo-pher Pepusch. Also participating in the enterprise were men of culture, such as the writer Jonathan Swift and William Hogarth, painter of the drawings of the spectacle (above).

♦ **A MODERN VERSION**
Bertoldt Brecht's *The Three Soldiers*, with music by Kurt Weill, was inspired by the work of John Gay (above).

The English public always loved a type of opera that was half sung and half recited. Italian opera, imported at the end of the 1600s, was initially judged as a "harmonious folly" precisely because it was sung from beginning to end. The arrival of Händel in London, in 1710, not only decreed Italian opera to be fashionable, but changed the history of English music. Theatrical life became greatly enriched. Beside the annals of opera also grew a popular theater, inventive and irreverent. In 1728 *The Beggar's Opera,* by the poet John Gay, was staged. It is a satire of political corruption, of high society, and of Italian music: it was a scandal, but it was also the greatest success of English theater.

♦ **COSTUMES**
The production of serious opera forced theaters to organize internal sewing laborato-ries. Popular the-ater recycled the rejected articles (hand-me-downs).

♦ **THE THEATERS**
Sustained by private funds, theaters in England began to turn into enterprises tied to a market logic.

♦ **THE WINGS**
These were mobile panels of the scenes; in back, behind the stage, the modern musical court came to life: divas, impresarios, true or improvised artists, tailors, and designers took part in the project from which the spectacle was born.

THE COMPOSERS
They arrived in England from all over Europe, attracted by high wages and by the relative independence of the liberal profession of the theater, without the conditions attached to service in a court.

♦ **THE KIT-CAT CLUB**
The most important trend of the Conservative Party (Whig). Its members, portrayed by Sir Godfrey Kneller (above) in the series *Portraits of the Kit-Cat Club,* supported Italian opera and were the object of Gay's satire.

♦ **WILLIAM HOGARTH** (1697–1764). A painter, he portrayed with critical irony the customs of English life. Among his targets were theatrical life and the opera world. He sympathized with John Gay for *The Beggar's Opera.*

♦ **JOHN GAY** (1685–1732) After the success of *The Beggar's Opera,* he wrote a sequel, *Polly,* but the work was blocked by the censors.

♦ **THE SINGERS**
In contrast to the very highly paid stars of Italian opera were actors of the popular theater who sang in a more uncouth manner.

♦ **THE IMPRESARIO**
The private manager that risks his fortunes in the opera and directly handles the wages of the singers and composers, without resorting to the mediation of the principals was born in London.

♦ **JONATHAN SWIFT** (1667–1745) The author of *Gulliver's Travels* closely followed the projects of the popular theater.

OPEN-AIR MUSIC

In addition to churches, palaces, and opera theaters, music was also performed in the open air, in gardens or in the piazzas. It was always present to solemnize great occasions, the celebration of a king's birthday, the end of a war, or even to accompany an entertainment spectacle such as fireworks. In order for open-air music to be effective, it was necessary for the orchestra to be notably large and to use those instruments with the most powerful sounds, such as trumpets and trombones. Händel wrote various works for such occasions and engaged orchestras containing up to 100 elements.

♦ **FIREWORKS**
Each year in London, in the public gardens or on the river, festivals were held with spectacles of fireworks. From 1736, these spectacles were often accompanied by music from Händel's *Atalanta.* In 1749, to celebrate England's victory in the War of the Spanish Succession, King George II (above) commissioned Händel to write the impressive *Fireworks Music.* Performed at Green Park on April 27, the music took a back seat to the spectacle of fire that destroyed the magnificent wooden pavilion from which the fireworks were shot. Below, fireworks shown in Diderot's *Encyclopedia.*

♦ **THE PUBLIC**
In London the fireworks were attended by enormous crowds. The king and the nobles were on platforms that were supported by scaffolding. The rest of the crowd wandered between the site of the spectacle and the nearby streets.

♦ **THE ORCHESTRA**
It was reinforced with instruments that were defined as "military," such as drums, kettledrums (timpani), trumpets, horns, trombones, and in general with a large number of wind instruments.

♦ **THE DIRECTORS**
During the festivity, the musical director followed the arrangements of the superintendent of the artillery and of the director of the fireworks.

7. THE LIFE OF BACH ♦ *The opportunity of directing the Weimar Orchestra presented itself in 1716, upon the death of the former director, Johann Samuel Drese. But Duke Wilhelm Ernst preferred to keep the position in the family and appointed Drese's son to the post. Disillusioned and irritated, Bach responded by accepting an appointment as musical director in a smaller court, that of Prince Leopold of Anhalt, in the nearby city of Köthen. The opposition of the Weimar court was violent: on December 2, 1717 Bach was arrested for failing to fulfill contractual obligations. In the end he departed for Köthen, where there was less call for sacred music and more demand for instrumental and entertainment music.* ⟫→

♦ **THE FIREWORKS**
These were introduced in Europe by China in the 1300s. Magnesium and aluminum powders produced the effects of light; saltpeter and potassium chloride, the colors.

WATER MUSIC
Händel wrote in 1715 a series of dances for the orchestra to be performed in boats, during King George II's voyages on the Thames. They were revised several times over the years.

♦ CATHERINE-WHEELS
The circles and Catherine-Wheels were the crucial part of the pyrotechnical spectacle: the beauty of the spectacle was judged on the variety of its shapes and colors.

♦ THE STOKERS (FIREWORKERS)
The superintendent of fireworks, generally chosen from the military artillery corps, commanded the artillery squads assigned to the spectacle.

♦ TELEMANN
Another famous *Water Music* is that written in 1723 by Georg Philipp Telemann (1681–1726), pictured above, one of the most original and productive composers of the German Baroque. The occasion was the centennial anniversary of the founding of the College of the Admiralty in the port city of Hamburg.

♦ THE ROCKETS
They outlined a luminous and colorful track rising into the air and bursting in a cascade of sparkles. The effect was simple but certain.

♦ THE PAVILIONS
They were magnificent constructions, usually of wood, designed by scene painters such as the Italian Roberto Servandoni, who had conceived the grandiose one for the festival of 1749.

THE MELODRAMA

The melodrama was the spectacle most frequently attended during the 1700s, and its language of choice was Italian, considered ideal for singing. The composers wrote arias and melodies that were ever more sought after and difficult to perform. The Italian singers—prima donnas or eunuchs—competed among themselves and obtained very high wages. Opera theaters often sustained very high production costs, as the bankruptcy of London's Royal Academy demonstrated. The most noble genre was serious opera, based on mythological themes or on ancient history. *Julius Caesar,* Händel's greatest operatic success, staged in 1724, is the most elaborate example.

♦ THE ROYAL ACADEMY OF MUSIC
In 1719 a group of London's nobles, lovers of Italian opera, created a stock company to manage Haymarket Theatre (above), entrusting Händel with its musical direction. The company's capital was fixed at 10,000 pounds sterling, with shares costing 200 pounds each. Among the underwriters was a Mrs. Pendarves, a friend of Händel's, and the members of the Kit-Cat Club. The contribution of the king, who participated with 1000 pounds, was actually very modest but sufficient to give the enterprise the name of Royal Academy of Music. Between 1720 and 1728, 487 performances were staged, 245 of which had the music of Händel. But the costs of the enterprise were exorbitant, and the tastes of the public were volatile. The success of popular opera, together with a financial scandal involving many of its members, forced the theater to close in 1728.

♦ CLEOPATRA
On stage was Francesca Cuzzoni, the highest paid soprano of the time.

♦ JULIUS CAESAR
In 1724 he was played by Senesino, one of the most famous eunuchs; Händel made him a divided figure: a warring spirit and a very sentimental one.

♦ NIRENO
Cleopatra's valet, he prepares the seduction scene: the Muses play while Cleopatra sits on high and sings the aria "V'adoro pupille."

♦ THE NINE MUSES
In Greek mythology the Muses protected the arts. Händel had them play in the scene to help Cleopatra seduce Julius Caesar.

♦ **CASTRATI AND PRIMA DONNAS**
Little boys with beautiful voices often underwent operations to remove their testicles. Consequently, during growth, the thoracic cavity became rounded, giving more power and reserves of breath to the lungs. The voice, moreover, remained clear and with an even greater range than a female one. Famous Italian castrati dominated the melodrama stage in the 1700s, from Francesco Bernardi, called the Senesino (the Little Sienese) (in the cartoon above), to Carlo Broschi, called Farinelli (below). They generally portrayed the heroic characters, while for the women, with sweeter and more sensual voices, were reserved the amorous roles, be they male or female.

♦ **THE AUDIENCE**
In the boxes reserved for the nobles there was a refreshment service. Admission for servants and domestics was free in the gallery, while the connoisseurs occupied a few rows in the orchestra. Behind them, standing, was the casual public.

♦ **THE ORCHESTRA**
In the melodrama the orchestra was generally large. Using a smaller one on the stage, Händel created intimacy in the amorous dialogue.

THE MUSICAL PRESS

Until the end of the 1600s, the printing of musical works was the exception rather than the rule. Typographical processes were particularly complicated, and the production costs were very high. Engraving, a new printing technique, was introduced in the Baroque Age, rendering the work more economical and allowing for the distribution of works of all kinds. Thus was born a market of musical editions requested both for private use and for the public performance of operas and concerts. A new rapport was established between composers and publishers. Those who, like Bach, did not adapt to the public's tastes, ended up giving publishers very few works and submitting works to scribes who copied them by hand.

♦ THE PUBLISHING INDUSTRY

Between 1600 and 1700 a very simple market logic was introduced: the melodrama made a profit when staged live, and instrumental music became profitable when sold as a printed edition (above, a page by Lully). Since melodramas still had a very limited diffusion in the area, common interests on the part of publishers and composers focused on the circulation of instrumental music. The concertos of Corelli and Vivaldi were among the successes of the time. The diffusion of their work was the basis of the prestige of the Italian style that was evidenced even in the concertos of Händel, another composer whose works sold well. Few, however, were the publications of Bach: a cantata or two and some didactic works, such as *The Well-Tempered Clavier.* Even Scarlatti's sonatas became commercialized in the 1700s under the title *Exercises for the Harpsichord.*

♦ PUBLISHERS

Estienne Roger in Amsterdam and John Walsh in London were the most important publishers of the Baroque Age. The former published mostly Italian music; the latter became Händel's exclusive publisher. They received the works of composers on assignment, and paid them based on the length of the assignment instead of sales.

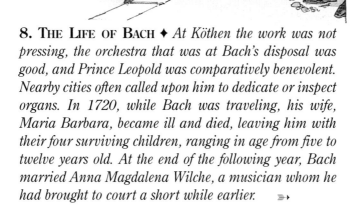

8. THE LIFE OF BACH ♦ *At Köthen the work was not pressing, the orchestra that was at Bach's disposal was good, and Prince Leopold was comparatively benevolent. Nearby cities often called upon him to dedicate or inspect organs. In 1720, while Bach was traveling, his wife, Maria Barbara, became ill and died, leaving him with their four surviving children, ranging in age from five to twelve years old. At the end of the following year, Bach married Anna Magdalena Wilche, a musician whom he had brought to court a short while earlier.* ⟫▸

♦ ENGRAVING
This is the incision of musical notes on copper plates, which in the 1600s replaced the more costly and laborious process of movable characters in wood.

Engraving allowed for speed and precision in the alignment of the notes, the words, and the pentagram (staff) that previously had to be done in three distinct stages.

♦ ESTIENNE ROGER
(1666–1722)
His legal battle against Pierre Mortier, who had reproduced works before Estienne Roger more economically, legally settled publishing rights (copyrights).

♦ THE WASHING OF THE FORMS
This took place in a container connected to a copper kettle and was done with potassium-based lye.

THE ORATORIO

At the beginning of the 1500s, Saint Philip Neri founded the Congregation of the Oratorio at the church of Saint Gerolamo of Charity in Rome, and had introduced a musical practice to reinforce the involvement of the faithful, especially the youth. The genre subsequently called oratorio came out of this initiative, and thus added to the history of sacred music the assigning of parts of the various protagonists to different voices. The effectiveness of this medium immediately attracted the attention of the Church's hierarchy as well as professional composers such as Giacomo Carissimi. The oratorio very closely imitated the language of the theater, basing itself on Bible stories and especially on the crucifixion of Jesus.

♦ THE ROMAN ORATORIO
Saint Philip Neri staged the sacred performances in Rome, at Santa Maria della Vallicella (above, the facade of the church) and in the oratory of Saint Gerolamo of Charity Church. At Easter, the events of the sacrifice of Jesus Christ were recounted musically: the parts of the characters were assigned to the youngsters of the oratory, and the youth who was best prepared musically was assigned the task of connecting the various episodes with a chanted reading of the sacred text. After Saint Philip, the oratorio in Rome was developed by Giacomo Carissimi (1605–1674), who rendered a Latin form, based mostly on stories from the Bible. The music was richer, the arias were more like those of opera, and the chorus was very simple. His masterpiece is *Jephte,* based on melodrama: that of a father who because of a promise has to sacrifice his own son.

♦ THE CHORUS
The chorus either gave voice to the sentiments of the faithful or else acted out the role of the crowd, but it could also be used more freely.

♦ SAINT PETER
The most human and the most tragic character for whom the most painful and intense arias are reserved, in many cases accompanied by a concert instrument.

♦ JESUS
In the sacred play, Jesus utters few words before Pilate and on the cross: His tone is solemn and the music is airy.

♦ EVANGELIST
This is the voice that intoned the sacred texts. The chant, like a recitative, required good vocal technique.

41

♦ THE ORCHESTRA
In the first Roman oratorios, it was very simple: a harpsichord and a few stringed instruments. When it was enlarged, dramatic effects were created with the instruments, such as the earthquake that shook the earth upon the death of Christ.

♦ THE ORATORIO IN EUROPE
Outside of Italy, the oratorio was promulgated during this same period, but in different styles. In France the most important composer was Marc-Antoine Charpentier (above, 1643–1704), a student of Carissimi in Rome and the only musician in Paris in a position to rival the authority of Lully. With Charpentier music occupied a great deal of space with respect to the text. The oratorio thus became less of a narrative and more an occasion of prayer and meditation in music. In Germany, on the other hand, the model adhered to was that of a staged narrative, but with the addition of an element typical of Lutheran music, the chant. In Germany, the Passion of Christ became, among other things, the dominant if not the exclusive theme of oratorios. A highly spectacular version developed in England, often with scenes and costumes, whose ultimate representative was Händel.

♦ CARISSIMI
Carissimi, accompanied by some prelates, participates as an observer during the performance of Saint Philip Neri's oratorios and works in their musical development.

THE PASSIONS

The Passion According to St. John and *The Passion According to St. Matthew* are among Bach's major works. Staged in Leipzig about 1725 and rearranged many times, they modified the model of the Italian oratorio according to the German tradition. The evangelist narrates the event with a recitative; the chorus participates, alternatively personifying the crowd and the church community; Jesus intones a melody barely hinted at with minimal instrumental accompaniment, a sign of the need to reflect in silent prayer. The arias of the soloists are intervals of meditation from which emerges the character of the *Passions:* Matthew's, more dramatic and human; John's, more spiritual.

✦ **MATTHEW**
His epistle begins with the incarnation of Christ; his symbol is therefore a winged man.

✦ **JOHN**
John's epistle is the one that is spiritually most elevated: his symbol, therefore, is an eagle.

✦ **THE SACRIFICE**
The Passion According to St. John does not concentrate on the experience of pain but on the divine plan that is behind Christ's sacrifice. The climax of the work are the words Jesus uttered on the cross: "It is finished."

✦ **THE HEAD**
Crowned with thorns, the head of Christ is the symbol of suffering. In *The Passion According to St. Matthew*— more sensitive to the portrayal of pain—a very beautiful chant reappears at times and always brings together in a lament the community of the faithful.

✦ **THE WOUNDS**
They symbolize the responsibility of man who, following his human nature, renounces the Lord; but

repentance can redeem him. An example of this is the pain of Saint Peter, the sentimental nucleus of the two *Passions.*

✦ **PITY**
The music of the *Passions* often points to this sentiment: to participate in this musical collection truly means to travel the road from compassion to salvation.

42

THE MUSICAL NARRATIVE OF THE PASSION OF CHRIST

From the evangelical narrative, the music recaptured some episodes with ample pauses for meditation: the last supper; Jesus' arrest; his interrogation; the participation of the crowd in condemning him; and the crucifixion, death, and the descent from the cross. With respect to the sacred chants, whose structure is very similar, the *Passions* are simpler and more communicative. Bach searched for symbolism and distributed chants, recitatives, and arias according to a precise geometry. But what moves the faithful is not the structure of the *Passions,* but rather their expressive power: the contrast between the dignity of Jesus and the agitation of His accusers, the simplicity of the chants and the beauty of the arias. Many series of paintings are dedicated to the Passion of Christ. Among these, at the beginning of modern painting, are those of Giotto. Giotto's 1. *The Last Supper*; 2. *The Capture*; 3. *The Flagellation*; 4. *The Way of the Cross*; 5. *The Crucifixion*; 6. *The Lament for the Crucified Christ*; frescos, 1302–1306; Padua, Chapel of the Scrovegni.

MUSICAL EDUCATION

The School of Saint Thomas at Leipzig, where Bach held the position of cantor (the person responsible for musical activities), offers an example of scholastic life and of the organization of basic musical studies during the Baroque Age. The school's regulations were very strict: only three vacation days a year, absolute discipline, corporal punishment on Fridays for infractions committed during the week, rationed food, and prayer recitation at various times of day. Students who were musically gifted enjoyed a few extra privileges. The cantor lived in the school building with his family: the tasks associated with his position occupied almost all of his time, but outside activities were not forbidden.

♦ **SCHOOL LIFE**
The School of Saint Thomas (above, in an engraving) was established as a school for poor children and was maintained by funds from the town of Leipzig, by private donations, and by money earned by musical groups for performances staged in addition to scheduled ones. The alarm rang at five in the morning in the summer and at six in the winter. Each student then had fifteen minutes to dress and prepare for prayer, bringing with him his own Bible. There was also prayer before and after each meal, during which there were readings from a chapter of the sacred scriptures. Among the punishments, inflicted for every minute infraction, the one most frequently administered was the fast. Below, a portrait of Matthias Gesner, rector of the school, who became a close friend of Bach.

♦ **THE CHURCH**
The school was next to the church of Saint Thomas and was originally its dependency. At left, the interior of the church.

9. THE LIFE OF BACH ♦ *Various factors convinced Bach to leave Köthen: the desire to begin composing sacred music once again, the crisis in his relationship with Prince Leopold, his determination to give his children a university education. The first order of business was to move to Hamburg, but Bach refused to pay a large sum of money to obtain the post of organist, one that he had won in a competition. The choice, therefore, was Leipzig, which offered him the position of cantor at the church of Saint Thomas. It was a less prestigious position than that of choir master at Köthen, but in Leipzig Bach found the stability he desired for himself and the opportunities that he wanted for his children: he moved in 1723.* ≫♦

♦ **THE BEDROOMS**
Bach, Anna Magdalena, and the children slept in three rooms on the second floor.

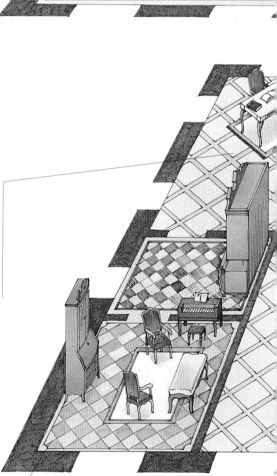

♦ **THE CANTOR'S QUARTERS**
After the restoration of 1732, the cantor had the use of twelve rooms on various floors of the school building.

♦ **BACH'S STUDY**
On the first floor, his rooms adjoined the school's: a library, a room in which to compose, and an antechamber to receive guests.

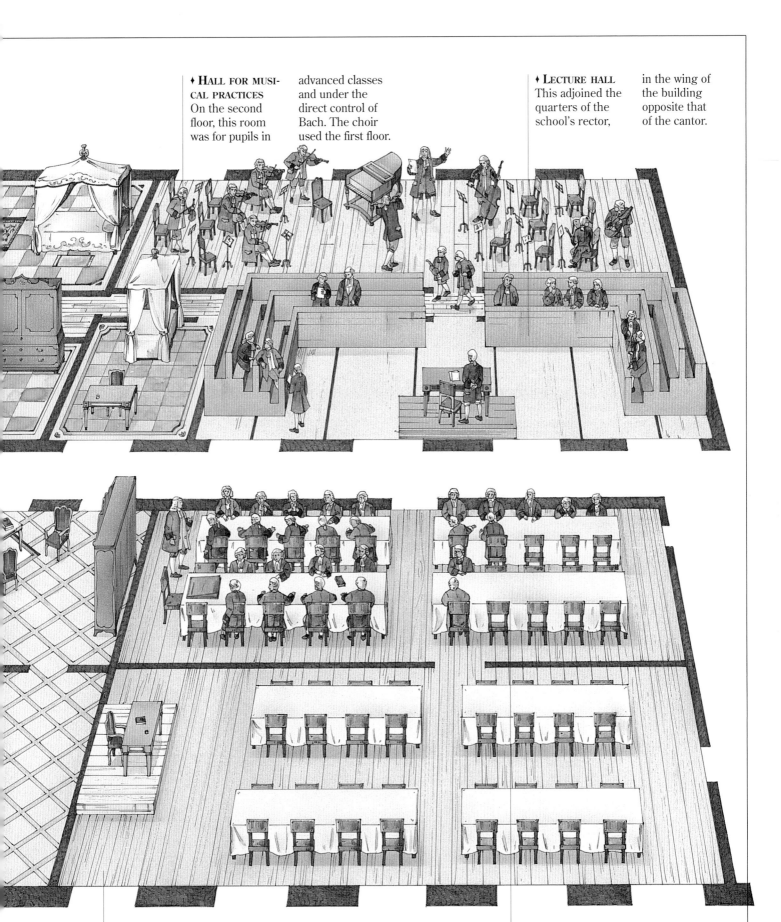

♦ **HALL FOR MUSI-CAL PRACTICES**
On the second floor, this room was for pupils in advanced classes and under the direct control of Bach. The choir used the first floor.

♦ **LECTURE HALL**
This adjoined the quarters of the school's rector, in the wing of the building opposite that of the cantor.

♦ **LOWER CLASSES**
There were three different levels, with studies in Latin and German. The choral exercises were guided by an older student.

♦ **UPPER CLASSES**
Even here there were three levels, but the students were only allowed to speak in Latin. These classes, less crowded, were for the school's boarders.

DAILY LIFE

In the Baroque Age, musicians could pursue an independent career only when they dedicated themselves to the melodrama, the only genre that opened the way to economic well-being. Those who, like Bach, did not write for the theater, could aspire to a position such as organist, teacher, or choir master, that is, director of the musical groups of a church or a court. At Leipzig, where he was musical director of the School of Saint Thomas, Bach supplemented his modest salary by preparing music for weddings and funerals, or else by offering his advice on the restoration and evaluation of the organs of the region.

♦ BACH'S WEEK
At Leipzig, Bach's workday (above, in a portrait of the era) began at 7:00 A.M., after which he had already dedicated one hour to prayers with his children and to the performance of a morning chant at home. On Mondays, Tuesdays, and Wednesdays, from 9:00 A.M. to 12:00 P.M., and on Fridays, from 12:00 P.M. to 1:00 P.M., he held singing lessons and instrumental exercises at the School of Saint Thomas. Thursday was his free day, while Saturday was dedicated to practicing for Sunday's singing. More than on Bach's salary, the family's standard of living depended on supplemental musical engagements for which Bach was called upon. Below, an 18th-century pocket watch.

♦ THE MORNING CHANT
In the Bach home, it was a tradition: there was singing before 7:00 A.M., but when guests were present this was often repeated in the evening, too. Sebastian was proud of having a chorus and a small orchestra in the family.

♦ THE OLDER SONS
Bach registered his older sons, Wilhelm Friedemann and Carl Philipp Emanuel, at the university. They remained in their father's house until about the age of twenty.

♦ CATHARINA DOROTHEA
Bach's firstborn did not marry, but instead raised her younger brothers and sisters.

10. THE LIFE OF BACH ♦ *Bach remained at Leipzig the rest of his life, without ever again changing jobs. He prepared music for all the sacred festivities, in spite of repeated conflicts with the municipal authorities and with the rector of Saint Thomas School. To honor his musical obligations, Bach often found himself revising works and materials he had already used in Weimar and Köthen. In the music written in Leipzig, there is a stratification of materials that shows the hand of Anna Magdalena, who helped her husband in transcribing them.* ⇒▸

♦ THE FURNISHINGS
The furniture was ordinary, but the musical instruments were numerous. The only valuable objects that Bach possessed were a glass goblet adorned with his initials and a snuff-box of agate and gold.

♦ THE DIARY OF ANNA MAGDALENA
When she became a widow, she wrote a brief domestic chronicle (at left, the title page) to convince the Leipzig authorities to grant her a fair pension. Anna Magdalena received, however, minimal help from the town and spent her last years in poverty, living with her two youngest children.

♦ MUSIC FOR THE HOME
Bach composed many didactic works for the members of his own family, a sign that he placed great importance on the musical education of his children. Most of these works were designed for Wilhelm Friedemann (above), Bach's oldest son and favorite child. He was only twelve years old when Bach dedicated the first book of *The Well-Tempered Clavier* to him, after already having written two other *Little Clavier Books* of study for the organ and harpsichord for him, among which also figure the fifteen *Inventions* in two or three voices. Another didactic work for domestic use was the one Bach completed in 1725 for his wife, *The Little Anna Magdalena Book* for the harpsichord and voice, with dance and suites in the French style, along with a couple of compositions by the very young Carl Philipp Emanuel, opportunely corrected by his father.

♦ MEALS
The family gathered together for morning and evening meals. Bach and his school-aged sons had their lunch at the cafeteria of Saint Thomas School.

♦ JOHANN CHRISTIAN
Bach's youngest musician son, born in 1735, was fifteen years old when his father died. He inherited three harpsichords and went to live with his brother, Carl Philipp Emanuel.

♦ THE FAMILY
Bach had twenty children: seven by his first wife, thirteen by his second. Ten of them reached adulthood. There were 34 years between the oldest and the youngest.

♦ ANNA MAGDALENA
Bach's second wife came from a family of musicians, had a beautiful soprano voice, and spent entire evenings copying her husband's music by candlelight and choosing the texts for the cantatas with him.

THE WELL-TEMPERED CLAVIER

Between 1600 and 1700, the development of instrumental music demanded a solution to a long-standing problem: establishing a general rule to tune instruments and to measure the distance between single sounds. The systems employed up to that time varied from region to region and favored the use of certain tonalities at the expense of others. It took Andreas Werckmeister to define the system called "uniform temper," which divides the musical octave into twelve equal parts, but it was Bach who disseminated it with the publication of the forty eight preludes and fugues of *The Well-Tempered Clavier.*

♦ **OPERA FOR THE HARPSICHORD**
The Well-Tempered Clavier is divided into two volumes published twenty-two years apart, in 1722 and 1744. Each volume consists of twenty-four preludes and fugues "of all the tones and semitones," as Bach wrote, thus a pair of compositions for every possible tonality in "major" and "minor" keys established by the tempered system. With this work Bach offered a very precious guide in the use of the most up-to-date harmonic theories, exploring their expressive potentialities, subjecting them to the rigorous discipline of the counterpoint, and offering an unparalled lesson in the technique of the keyboard instruments. Above, a German-made harpsichord; below, the quill that plucks the strings of the harpsichord.

♦ **THE TEMPER**
The German organist and theorist Andreas Werckmeister (1645–1706) defined it as "uniform" because it equalized the intonation of semitones and allowed tuning in a uniform manner the instruments of fixed sound, such as the keyboard instruments.

♦ **THE NOTES**
The names of the sounds are seven (Do, Re, Mi, Fa, Sol, La, Ti), but each note can be altered, that is, lowered a half tone with a mark called a flat, or raised a half tone with a mark called a sharp.

♦ **THE TUNING FORK**
Invented at the beginning of the 1700s, it is a tool that, vibrating, produces a fixed sound, the basis of every tuning. Today the champion is "La," tuned on a frequency of 440 hertz per second. In the Baroque Age, the measure was less precise and the frequencies were generally lower.

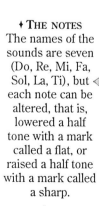

C Major or Do Major

F Major or Fa Major

A Minor or La Minor

G Major or Sol Major

D Minor or Re Minor

E Minor or Mi Minor

B Flat Major or Ti Flat Major

G Minor or Sol Minor

B Minor or Ti Minor

D Major or Re Major

E Flat Major or Mi Flat Major

C Minor or Do Minor

F Sharp Minor or Fa Sharp Minor

A Major or La Major

A Flat Major or La Flat Major

F Minor or Fa Minor

C Sharp Minor or Do Sharp Minor

E Major or Mi Major

B Flat Minor or Ti Flat Minor

D Sharp Minor (E Flat Minor) or Re Sharp Minor (Mi Flat Minor)

G Sharp Minor or Sol Sharp Minor

D Flat Major or Re Flat Major

B Major or Ti Major

F Sharp Major (G Flat Major) or Fa Major (Sol Flat Major)

✦ Tonalities

The foundation of modern harmony, tonalities indicate the order that governs the sounds within a composition (the internal sounds of a composition). In the tempered system there are twenty-four tonalities: twelve major ones and twelve minor ones. Together they can be represented by a circle.

✦ The octave

It is the distance between two equal sounds, but of different pitch. The tempered system divides the octave in twelve equal semitones. This division corresponds to the keyboard in a series of twelve white and black keys, one for each semitone.

✦ The Goldberg Variations

Tradition has it that one of Bach's students, Johann Gottlieb, a good harpsichord player in the service of Count Keyserlingk, had asked his teacher for a composition to play at night to alleviate the count's terrible insomnia. The anecdote is fanciful, but has popularized a work that is among the most complex of Bach's entire production. The *Goldberg Variations* (above, the title page) begins with a theme divided in two parts, which then develop into thirty beautiful variations that elaborate the theme according to the most diverse possibilities of the counterpoint, often rendering it unrecognizable to the ear or hiding it in the bass line, between the folds of the harmony. In the precise geometry of The *Goldberg Variations,* Bach brought together two characteristics of Baroque music: the search for variety and respect for unity.

CONCERTS AT CAFÉS

♦ TABLE MUSIC
Telemann published in Hamburg in 1733 an ample collection of suites, overtures, sonatas, and other orchestral music. Table music was not really destined to accompany banquets, but was included, rather, in a commercial genre that called to mind the type of music that was performed and preferred in the cafés by the Collegia Musica. Telemann boasted a great familiarity with this genre (below, a concert by students in an engraving of the period), given that he had founded many of them in Germany and continued to direct them even in Hamburg, where he lived from 1721 until his death in 1767. Above, the interior of a Leipzig café in a print of the period.

At the beginning of the 1700s, cafés became very lively gathering places, frequented by the bourgeoisie—the emerging class—but not disdained by the aristocracy. In the cafés people met, discussed the events of the day, gossiped, and read newspapers from all over Europe. In some, especially those with large outdoor verandas, people even listened to music. Private groups of citizens, in fact, organized high-level orchestras. These Collegia Musica, performed in public convivial music and even concerts of major importance. For eleven years, from 1729 to 1740, Bach directed the prestigious Collegium Musicum of forty pieces in Leipzig, founded by Telemann in 1702.

THE COLLEGIA MUSICA
These were associations of dilettante musicians (mostly bourgeoisie students) that dedicated themselves to the performance of orchestral and vocal music. Professionals such as Telemann greatly elevated the quality of these groups and regulated their activities with actual concert seasons.

♦ PERIODICALS
The cafés put at the disposal of their patrons periodicals of poetry, science, and current events that at that time kept all of Europe informed of the latest news.

♦ **IN LEIPZIG**
During the summer, the Helwig and Zimmermann cafés had a rich, open-air concert season: on their verandas, in the afternoons or in the evenings, the Collegia Musica held concerts. In the winter, people went to the Lehmann Café, in the market square.

♦ **THE CAFÉ'S CANTATA**
At the Zimmermann Café (above, in a print of the time) in 1734, Bach arranged the performance of a cantata poking fun at the influence that drink had assumed over the female public. The text was written by the poet Picander and reported the argument between a father and his daughter, a bass voice and a soprano voice, respectively, with a tenor portraying the voice of the narrator. The father admonishes his daughter for her rabid consumption of coffee, but she does not allow herself to be dissuaded and even inserts into the contract of her future marriage a clause which obliges her husband to permit her to drink coffee at will. The *Coffee Cantata*, which is catalogued in Bach's works as BWV 211, concludes with three choral voices proclaiming that since grandmothers and mothers drink coffee, it is impossible to blame daughters if they love it more.

♦ **THE PUBLIC**
With respect to the cultured aristocrats who listened to music in their palaces, the bourgeoisie public was less knowledgeable, but more curious and sensitive to musical innovations.

♦ **FASHION**
The distribution of periodicals prescribed the fashions of the time.

In the cafés, tobacco became popular, generally smoked in long brierwood pipes.

11. THE LIFE OF BACH ♦ *In 1729 Johann Matthias Gesner, a connoisseur of music and admirer of Bach, was elected rector. Together he and Bach established an excellent sodality, in which the musician could even work outside the school, assuming the direction of the most important Collegium Musicum of Leipzig. In 1734, however, Gesner was called to the University of Göttingen and a rector was appointed in his place, Johann August Ernesti, who did not consider the role of music in the school important. A period of harsh disputes began for Bach.* ⟫♦

THE AGE OF FREDERICK II

The end of the Thirty Years' War had made Brandenburg a strategically important region, especially in respect to powerful Sweden, with whom it was involved in a dispute over control of the Baltic Sea coasts. In the second half of the 1600s, Brandenburg strengthened its army enormously and conquered the territories that eventually formed the Kingdom of Prussia, with its capital at Berlin—the first unitarian state of large size in German territory. From 1740 to 1786, Prussia was governed by Frederick II, an enlightened sovereign, a patron of the arts, and an excellent musician. There began an epoch of important social reforms, but Prussia based its solidity on the organization and power of its army.

♦ BETWEEN ARMY AND REFORM
Frederick William, the father of Frederick II, had been the instigator of the military reinforcement that in a few years had transformed Prussia into a powerful kingdom, enabling it to conquer new territories. Frederick II (above, 1712–1786) did not abandon this policy, and within just three months of his installation he embarked on a series of wars that occupied the first twenty years of his reign. This state of continual mobilization increased the political power of the army and of the landed nobility that financed him. On the other hand, Frederick II introduced in Prussia vanguard social reforms: a reorganization of the bureaucracy and the courts, the advancement of agriculture, the establishment of a mandatory elementary education, and the founding of the Academy of Sciences based on the French model.

♦ THE ROYAL PALACE OF SANS-SOUCI
At Potsdam, in the lakes zone situated a few kilometers from the city of Berlin, Frederick II had built a grandiose royal palace called Sans-Souci, whose gardens equaled those of Versailles in beauty.

♦ POETRY
The king composed poetry: if he received an inspiration during a walk, he would dictate the verses to a scribe.

♦ FREDERICK II
Against the wishes of his father, he secretly studied music with borrowed money. After his ascent to the throne, he acquired from Silbermann fifteen pianos that he kept in various rooms of the splendid royal palace Sans-Souci.

♦ **THE FORTEPIANO (PIANO)**
This is the name of the instrument that improves upon the harpsichord.

♦ **MECHANISMS**
A lute-maker shows the king the quill and the hammer that, in the harpsichord and piano, respectively, pluck and strike the strings to produce sound.

♦ **THE FLUTE**
Frederick II studied flute with the virtuoso and composer Johann Joachim Quantz, a permanent guest at Sans-Souci.

THE MUSICAL OFFERING

On May 7, 1747 the elderly Bach went to Potsdam, a guest of his son Carl Philipp Emanuel, and was granted an audience with Frederick II while the court orchestra was about to begin its customary Sunday evening concert. The king, familiar with Bach's fame, approached the piano and played a composition, requesting his guest to expand it into a fugue. Bach astounded the audience by improvising one in six voices, *The King's Composition (Tema del Re)*. The king's original composition seemed to Bach so beautiful that he worked on it later and dedicated it to Frederick II. It was entitled *The Musical Offering*. It is a beautiful example of Bach's later style, characterized by a refined taste for rational construction and the ancient techniques of polyphony, the fruit of a vision that exalts the speculative aspect of music.

♦ THE OPUS
Published the first time in September of 1747, with only 100 copies by the publisher Breitkopf, *The Musical Offering* (above, the frontispiece) was conceived as an elaboration of *The King's Composition (Thema Regium)*. It used the most ample repertory possible of musical configurations, for a maximum of three instrumental parts: flute—in homage to the king—violin, and basso ostinato (harpsichord and bass or cello). In the work there are canons and fugues of exceptional difficulty and astounding virtuosity, just as there is an alternation of solo parts and passages with more instruments that demonstrate the lighter style that was fashionable in the court of Potsdam. To indicate the fugues, Bach used a term already obsolete at the time, *Ricercar* (to search, seek, investigate), to convey the erudite and academic character of the music and his connection with the more austere and faraway tradition from what was then fashionable.

♦ IMPROVISATION
It is pivotal to the performance techniques of Baroque music. Those of Bach on the keyboard were famous for their rigor and complexity.

♦ THE COMPOSITION
Improvised by the king, it has an irregular rhythm, complicated by notes that are not included in its fundamental tonality.

♦ PIANO
Years before Bach was disillusioned by Silbermann's instrument: the new model tested at Potsdam satisfied him.

♦ SEBASTIAN
The art and science of music became one in his last rich productions.

♦ **THE ELABORATION**
This composition worked with a variation of the harmony, the distance of the counterpoint, and the melodic flourish. These three levels were called disposition, expansion, and ornamentation respectively.

♦ **THE METHOD OF COMPOSITION**
Bach did not normally compose at the keyboard, but annotated his melodic ideas directly on the staff that he only later verified on the instrument. The keyboard was only his starting point when the music was improvised.

♦ **THE MUSIC ROOM**
The work of the architect Georg W. Knoblesdorff; it was one of the jewels of the Sans-Souci royal palace.

♦ **THE BERLIN SCHOOL**
In homage to the tastes of the king, a musical school was founded between the royal palace at Potsdam and the city of Berlin that was attentive to the values of the past and in particular to the counterpoint, a technique decidedly on the decline in an epoch in which melodic and sentimental music was preferred. The school followed Händel's style more than Bach's. Händel's work was considered closer to the modern sensibility of sentimental expression. Baron Gottfried van Swieten (above, 1733–1803) belonged to the Berlin School. He was a rich patron who at the end of the century, in Vienna, conveyed his passion for counterpoint to his protégés, first among them Mozart (below) and the young Beethoven.

♦ **JOHANN PHILIPP KIRNBERGER** (1721–1783)
Court composer at Potsdam and once a student of Bach, he admired the manner in which his teacher had boldly elaborated on a fugue of six voices of the complicated *Thema Regium*.

♦ **THE KING'S ORCHESTRA**
In 1747, it consisted of forty elements, though not all were regularly involved in the Sunday evening musical performances. They were directed by Johann Joachim Quantz (1697–1773), who was very skilled at almost all the principal instruments and entrusted with the task of writing new flute music for the king.

♦ **CARL PHILIPP EMANUEL**
A dependent of the king, he always participated in the Sunday evening concerts. In Berlin he associated with men of letters and philosophers of the Lessing circle.

MUSIC AND SCIENCE

When it comes to music, one may consider either the feelings it conveys or the rules with which it is written. The science academies of the 1600s and 1700s adopted the latter point of view and studied music with mathematical and geometrical tools. One of Bach's students, Lorenz Christoph Mizler, founded the Society for Musical Sciences in Leipzig. Its members included Händel, Telemann, and Bach himself. According to the society's bylaws, the musicians had to present a theoretical work each year. Bach did not complete *The Art of the Fugue* in time, the most complex work of his entire body of work. Published posthumously, it was read and commented on by his colleagues in a celebrated meeting.

♦ THE ART OF THE FUGUE
Conceived as music to read and meditate upon, Bach did not specify any instruments. All the possible forms of the fugue are present: straight or reversed, mirrored or simple, double or triple. *The Art of the Fugue* is incomplete: blindness prevented Bach from going beyond a triple-time fugue that hides among its themes the letters B-A-C-H: in German they correspond to the notes Ti flat, La, Do, and Ti natural. Above, Bach's seal.

♦ THE PORTRAITS
Each member had to furnish an oil portrait of himself. Händel's was added in 1745, the year he joined the society.

♦ CHRISTOPH MIZLER
The Society for Musical Sciences was founded by him in 1738 and ceased its activities in 1754.

♦ CARL PHILIPP EMANUEL BACH
He added a chant to the end of *The Art of the Fugue* that tradition says his father dictated to him on his deathbed.

♦ THE PHILOSOPHY
In their work, the musicians used as a model the theories of the philosopher Christian Wolff (1679–1754), an enlightened German.

♦ **THE CREST**
Hidden in the pattern are the initials of Bach— J S B—as well as other arithmetical symbols based on numbers corresponding to the letters in his complete name.

♦ **THE LIBRARY**
It already housed two prior academic submissions of Bach's: *Canonic Variations* for the organ and *The Musical Offering.* "Musical Library" was also the title of the monthly bulletin in which the society published reports of its activities and confronted thorny theoretical problems.

♦ **RAMEAU**
The union of music and science was also widespread outside of Germany, and was not only concerned with the mathematical aspects of the counterpoint, but primarily with the laws of harmony. Jean-Philippe Rameau (above, 1683–1733), the most important French composer of opera after Jean-Baptiste Lully, published in 1722 a *Treatise of Harmony,* which is still used today and is based on a rigorous mathematical interpretation not only of sounds, but also of nature. Rameau contended that the melody depends on performance and harmony: as a result he studied the shapes of chords, their similarities and differences, and established with physical and mathematical criteria the difference between consonance and dissonance within a tonality. His works were a model for French musical theater.

♦ **THE EDITIONS**
The Art of the Fugue was published in two editions, in 1751 and 1752, but did not meet with great success: in five years, less than 50 copies were sold.

12. THE LIFE OF BACH ♦ *The routine of Bach's life was interrupted in 1749 because of an eye illness, which in a short time weakened his general state of health. In 1750 he was operated on twice for cataracts by a famous English surgeon passing through Leipzig, John Taylor. The operations, however, were not successful. Bach became progressively more blind and continued working only by dictating music to his children and closest students. He died on July 28, 1750, leaving his musical testament,* The Art of the Fugue *incomplete.* ➠➧

THE CHILDREN

Of Bach's ten children who reached adulthood, four became musicians and had a principal role in the musical life of the 1700s, to the degree that by the end of the century their fame obscured that of their father. Educated in music at home by Sebastian, they all had an excellent preparation as organ and harpsichord virtuosos, as well as a solid familiarity with the rigorous style of the counterpoint. The typical formation of the Protestant organist inhibited them from performing melodrama; they were able to appreciate it, but not implement it. Only the youngest, Johann Christian, barely fifteen years old when his father died, succeeded in freeing himself from this subjugation and, having settled in England, worked a great deal both in the theater as well as in the burgeoning symphonic genre.

♦ JOHANN CHRISTOPH FRIEDRICH
(1732–1795)
He was responsible his entire life for the chamber music of the Count of Schaumburg-Lippe, in the city of Bückenburg.

WILHELM FRIEDEMANN
(1710–1784)
"Friede," Sebastian's oldest son and favorite child, was also the most musically gifted. He was greatly inhibited by his insecure and introverted personality, which caused grave misunderstandings with his superiors. He was the greatest organist of his generation, and he had ambitions of becoming a cultured musician, as well as an expert in mathematics and philosophy. He worked as a musician in Dresden and Halle and attempted an independent profession as a teacher, a position in which he was welcomed in Berlin by the sister of Frederick II, Anna Amalie. However, he did not get along with the court composer, Johann Philipp Kirnberger, and ended up being fired, and was forced to sell his father's manuscripts in order to survive. His music for the harpsichord and his cantatas demonstrate the originality as well as the inconsistency of his genius.

♦ JOHANN CHRISTIAN
(1735–1782)
At the age of nineteen, he moved to Italy following his love of a singer. Upon his arrival in England, in 1762, he was already a famous musician.

♦ THEATRICAL LIFE
Even before he was drawn to operatic music, Johann Christian Bach was attracted to the life of the theater.

♦ MOZART
He played in public with Johann Christian Bach in London in 1762 and considered Bach's style decisive for the maturation of his own musical style.

♦ **CARL F. ABEL**
An old friend of
the family, he pro-
duced, together
with Christian,
the concertos
Bach-Abel, the
most important
in London.

♦ **COLOMBA MATTEI**
Director of the
King's Theatre,
she invited Chris-
tian to London as
theater composer
and lived with him
for a year.

♦ **CECILIA GRASSI**
A soprano, she
arrived in London
after Johann Chris-
tian, and married
him in 1782. Upon
his death, she
returned to Italy.

♦ **CARL PHILIPP
EMANUEL**
(1714–1788)
In the late 1700s,
when the name
Bach was men-
tioned, it mainly
referred to
Emanuel, the
second son of
Sebastian. His
music was a bril-
liant synthesis
of the modern
melodic style and
the rigorous lan-
guage of the
great German
tradition: it was
a decisive contri-
bution to the
formation of the
music of Haydn
and Beethoven.
He began to work
for Frederick II in
1736, two years
before Frederick
ascended the
throne. At court
he was greatly
appreciated, but
also the lowest
paid musician. In
1768 he moved to
Hamburg to
obtain a raise in
salary. Here he
was superinten-
dent of the Latin
school, the
Johanneum,
holding the same
position that his
father had held at
Leipzig. Attentive
custodian of his
father's memory,
he wrote an
important treatise
on the method
of playing the
harpsichord.

LEGACY

After the death of Bach, interest in his music diminished rapidly. One reason for this change in taste was a distancing of the sensibility of the public from the harsher and spiritual focuses of his work. Also, during his life, only a small portion of his work was published, which limited its circulation. The conservation of the Bach treasury was entrusted to his children and a tight circle of acquaintants. Things changed in the 1800s, after the performance of *The Passion According to St. Matthew,* conducted in 1829 in Berlin by Felix Mendelssohn Bartholdy. But the size of the orchestra was so enlarged, the instruments and the manner of performing the music so changed, that the historic Bach almost disappeared behind the idealized portrait that the subsequent epoch handed down.

♦ **THE EDITIONS OF THE WORKS**
A great part of Bach's handwritten legacy was dispersed by his heirs. Even Carl Philipp Emanuel, the most attentive in conserving his father's memory, was forced to sell the sixty very heavy zinc plates upon which were engraved *The Art of the Fugue.* At the beginning of the 1800s, a few editions of Bach's works were printed, but the collection was quite incomplete. In 1850, the centennial anniversary of Bach's death, the complete collection of Bach's work was printed under the auspices of the Bach Society in Leipzig. The undertaking, which lasted fifty years, was completely revised as the *New Bach Edition,* which was printed in 1954 by the publisher Bärenreiter according to the most up-to-date methods of research available at the time. Above and below, two of Bach's manuscript pages.

♦ **THE HALL**
Mendelssohn conducted *The Passion According to St. Matthew* at the Singakademie of Berlin, an auditorium that seats more than 1000 people. The grand modern orchestra filled up the great acoustic spaces of the new halls.

♦ **FEMALE VOICES**
When sacred music began to be performed in concert halls, "white" voices were replaced by women, both in the chorus and for the solos.

♦ **FELIX MENDELSSOHN BARTHOLDY** (1809–1847)
One of the greatest exponents of Romantic music, he was an impassioned devotee of older music. In addition to modifying the orchestration, he introduced deletions and additions in his own hand to the *Passion.*

◆ **BRASS INSTRUMENTS**
Horns, trumpets, and trombones acquire greater intonation, power, and precision in the modern orchestra thanks to the addition of cylinders, pistons, and valves effected by German artisans in the first decade of the 1800s.

◆ **THE FIRST BIOGRAPHY**
In 1802 the composer Johann Nikolaus Forkel (above, 1749–1818) published the first biography of Bach. For this work Forkel collected the precious testimonies of Bach's sons, Wilhelm Freidemann and Carl Philipp Emanuel.

◆ **PHILOLOGY**
In this century, the rediscovery of Bach's work was supported by research techniques that have eliminated from the musical scores the many arbitrary interventions used by curators of the 19th-century editions. Since the 1960s, a return to the type of orchestra used in the time of Bach has occurred, that is, to the instruments that in the intervening years have been modified or have disappeared, such as the viola da gamba, above.

◆ **STRINGED INSTRUMENTS**
The acoustic bass disappears in the modern orchestra, replaced by the cello, which now is supported by a metal tip, and double-basses are perfected.

BACH'S WORK

Bach is the first composer for whom it was necessary to compile, over the course of the 19th century, a complete catalogue of works. No doubt furthering this necessity was the discovery that the music of Beethoven, Mendelssohn, and the Romantics in general owed a great deal to Bach. The decisive factor, however, came from the very deficient state of Bach's musical legacy. While he was alive, very few of his compositions were submitted to publishers. His work was mainly conserved in manuscripts that were later dispersed by his heirs, tampered with by other composers, and confused by the hand of Bach himself, who did not hesitate to reutilize the same music in different contexts over the course of many years. The "Bach Society," founded in Germany in 1850, pro-

moted an edition of his works that kept track of all the traceable manuscripts. The task took forty-nine years, until 1899. In 1950 the Bach Society published a "New Bach Edition," still in print, based on many newly discovered materials and on the most current analysis methods available to establish the chronology of the individual musical pieces. From the first "Bach Edition," the "New Bach Edition" kept the numeration, accompanied by the initials BWV (corresponding to the German "Bach Werke Verzeichnis") and the subdivision by genre, that does not keep track of the chronology and touches upon practically every musical form practiced during the Baroque Age, with the exception of the melodrama, the only genre to which Bach did not dedicate even one composition.

THE SACRED CANTATAS

This is the most extensive chapter in the Bach catalogue. Two hundred completed cantatas have been handed down, with about another twenty in a fragmented or incomplete state. From a chronological point of view, they span Bach's entire career: from cantata **BWV 106**, called *Actus Tragicus* and written in 1707, to the second version of cantata **BWV 195**, *Dem Gerechten muss das Licht immer wieder aufgehen (The Just Must Always Be Guided by the Light)*, completed between 1747 and 1748. Depending on the occasions for which they were written, the cantatas have an instrumentation and an internal division of varied parts, in addition to a writing that, especially in the case of the arias, is very reminiscent of the lyric operas of that time. In church they were performed as a complement to the sermon; as a result, they either have a more developed narrative part, usually summed up in the recitatives, or they limit themselves to a series of arias and choruses (chants). Bach even wrote many cantatas without recitatives, for example **BWV 182**, *Himmelskönig sei Wilkommen (Blessed Be Thou, O King of Heaven)*, **BWV 12**, *Weinen Klagen, Sorgen Zagen (Cry, Pain, Fear, and Trembling)*; **BWV 172** *Erschallet, ihr Lieder, erklinget, ihr Saiten (Expand Yourselves O Chants, Resound Strings)*. This last one has the most ample structure: four solo voices (soprano, contralto, tenor, and bass); a chorus of four voices; trumpets, kettledrums, flute, oboe, strings (as always, first and second violins, violas, cellos, and bass), in addition to a basso ostinato done by the organ, cello, and bassoon. Cantata **BWV 182**, on the other hand, is the one with the most compact orchestration: three solo voices (contralto, tenor, and bass); a chorus of four voices; flute, strings, and basso ostinato.

The cantatas with recitatives are the major part of this work. Even here, Bach utilized many different structures. The most important is the one tried out in Leipzig in 1730, in which he combined the texts of Protestant chants and those of modern spiritual poetry *(Kirchenlieder)* with a composition technique that is rigorously mathematical. Cantata **BWV 137**, *Loben den Herren*

(Praise the Lord), and **BWV 112**, *Der Herr ist mein getreuer Hirt (The Lord Is My Good Shepherd)* can serve as models of this elaborate musical structure. With regard to the richness of the instrumentation we can again cite cantata **BWV 101**, *Nimm von uns, Herr, du treuer Gott*, while for vocal virtuosity **BWV 51**, *Jauchzet Gott in allen Landen (God Be Praised Everywhere)* stands out. Among the most famous we find cantata **BWV 147**, *Herz und Mund und Tat und Leben (Heart and Mouth and Action and Life)*.

SECULAR CANTATAS

This is the most deficient area of Bach's work, the most difficult to reconstruct, and the one that, if completed, could have perhaps showed a different aspect of the composer, one who adhered more closely to the prevalent styles of the day and who celebrated the joy of living, one less tied to the cliché of the composer concerned solely with religious meditation. It is, however, important to note that the genre of the "secular cantata" does not completely exclude a religious discussion: "secular" referred to all music that was not used in Sunday Masses, but that could have been performed for other liturgical occasions and in other settings, for example, weddings and funerals. This is the case with the famous and splendid *Trauerode (Funereal Ode)*, cantata **BWV 198**, written for the funeral ceremony of Christiane Eberhardine of Saxony, or of cantata **BWV 216**, *Vergnünte Pleissenstadt*, a matrimonial work from which came down to us through only the vocal parts. The majority of Bach's cantatas are dedicated to the celebration of birthdays, name days, or festivals celebrating a new year. The only one that truly emerges from a nonceremonial use is the so-called *Coffee Cantata (Kaffee-Kantate* **BWV 211**), of 1734. It is a kind of mini-drama written for a performance in one of the Leipzig cafés, probably the Zimmermann, but it is also a work that reveals the not so marginal interest cultivated by Bach in the dramatic genre outside of the theater of opera, as evidenced by other cantatas of a similar nature, such as *Vereinigte Zwietracht* **BWV 207**, composed for the appointment of Gottlieb Korrte in 1726 as a university professor.

GREAT SACRED WORKS

Next to the cantatas, in the Bach catalogue of works the Masses with a Latin text, the oratorios, and the passions stand out. They are works that are clearly different from each other in the organization of their musical parts, used within a religious setting. What they have in common is a monumental concept that pushes to the limit the performance possibilities of the time, apart from a writing style that is more communicative than that of the cantatas. If, indeed, these are the laboratory of Bach's art, in these great sacred works he approaches more closely that which he knows and offers a technique that is less rigorous, less experimental, and more direct and accessible to the ear. This is true above all for the *Passions*, great frescoes that narrate the events of the martyrdom and crucifixion of Jesus. The basic texts are taken from the gospels; to these are added spiritual poems and chants that serve, respectively, to give voice to both the individual and collective meditation of the faithful. Bach probably wrote four or five of them, almost all for the Church of Saint Thomas at Leipzig. Only two have remained: *The Passion According to St. Matthew* **BWV 244** and *The Passion According to St. John* **BWV 245**. The first is more dramatic, almost theatrical, and has moments that are extremely moving, such as the aria of the forgiveness of Peter or the chorus *O Hauptt voll Blut und Wunden (O Head Filled with Blood and Wounds)*. *The Passion According to St. John* is more austere, as is the text of the gospel that, with respect to that of Matthew, is more meditative, more narrative. Not lacking, however, even in this *Passion*, arias and moments of great expressive impact, such as the words *Zerfließe mein Herze (Free Yourself, My Heart)* sung by the soprano. But the true protagonist, from the most powerful introductory page, is the chorus, the geometric center of the entire musical construction. However, since the goal of the *Passions* is that of moving the faithful and involving them in the suffering of Christ, Bach avoids musical technicalities in both and chooses a style that is simpler than that of the cantatas. Here, even the fugue and the counterpoint serve to recount and represent a sacred event; they therefore have value not only as a system of organization of sounds, but are colored with a new expressive hue.

The chorus is also the principal component in the *Mass in B Minor* **BWV 232**, the masterpiece of Bach's sacred work. It is a composite work, assembled by Bach in 1749, almost at the end of his life, with musical parts written over a span of almost thirty years—from 1724, date of the *Sanctus*, the oldest part of the Mass, to 1749, the year in which the *Agnus Dei* was completed. The Lutheran Church allowed the use of Latin in the Mass, but had different traditions with respect to the Catholic Church. For example, it did not concede that the entire Mass should be set to music, but only one of the parts of the so-called *Ordinarium*, that is, the text that is repeated each Sunday and that does not vary according to the calendar's holy days. These include the *Kyrie*, the *Gloria*, the *Sanctus*, the *Benedictus*, and the *Agnus Dei*. Bach probably decided to write so ample a Mass thinking not so much of its "confessional" use—Lutheran or Catholic—but as a profession of faith that transcends the conflicts between churches. Musically, this religious unity is reflected in the synthesis of "ancient" and "modern" styles, that is, polyphonic and airy, contrapuntal and melodic, all subjected to a most refined elaboration and empowered by a very rich orchestra. Below is the division of the *Mass in B Minor*:

First Part: *Kyrie* and *Gloria*, in all, eleven musical episodes united under the title of *Missa*.

Second Part: *Symbolum Nicenum*, that is, the *Credo*, divided into nine musical episodes.

Third Part: *Sanctus*, a sole, compact element, the oldest part of the Mass.

Fourth Part: *Osanna, Benedictus, Agnus Dei,* and *Dona Nobis Pacem,* four musical episodes.

In all, there are twenty-five episodes, or musical "numbers," with a distinct prevalence of choruses (sixteen) with respect to the solo arias (six) and duets (three).

Among the oratorios stands out *Weihnachts Oratorium (Christmas Oratorio)* **BWV 248**, a six-part cycle based on the gospel narration that is reminiscent of the *Passions*, even though it is more static and less dramatic with respect to these last ones.

CHANTS AND OTHER SACRED VOCAL WORKS

An impressive quantity of revisions of Lutheran chants and other spiritual chants is sprinkled throughout Bach's catalogue and completes the portion of his sacred works that contain vocal parts. Worth mentioning are the six very beautiful motets for a chorus "a cappella" (that is, for a chorus alone, without instrumental accompaniment or with only a basso ostinato) **BWV 225–230**.

COMPOSITIONS FOR KEYBOARD INSTRUMENTS

Bach wrote music for the organ and the harpsichord that was designed for the most part to be performed either in church—such as the many chants for the organ—or as exercises for his children, such as the various notebooks entitled *Clavier-Übung* and able to be played on either instrument.

Among the works especially designed for the harpsichord are the *Inventions,* short compositions that greatly deviate from their original didactic purpose and that Bach compiled in a single booklet in 1723. The various suites, successions of dances originating from different European traditions and—depending upon the style upon which the introductory piece (the overture) was conceived—are considered English or French. A major work that can be said to reflect European music is *The Well-Tempered Clavier,* two books completed about 1742, each of which consists of twenty-four preludes and fugues, a pair of compositions for each of the tonalities that define the field of modern harmony, otherwise known as the "tempered" system that was affirming itself exactly during Bach's time. Most important, then, are the *Goldberg Variations* **BWV 988**: an aria is first presented, then subjugated to an elaboration that aims at the bass line and presents thirty successive variations of very different character, from the most virtuosic and brilliant to the most somber and meditative.

Among the compositions for the organ, in addition to the numerous *Toccatas and Fugues* that belong to Bach's first creative period, are the so-called *Canonic Variations* **BWV 769**, written between 1746 and 1747. Based on a Lutheran aria derived, in turn, from a popular chant, they are among the densest and most fascinating works of Bach's final years.

OTHER SOLO INSTRUMENTS AND CHAMBER MUSIC

In addition to those works written for keyboard instruments, Bach also wrote for other solo instruments, which, when considered with his other compositions, have contributed to the establishment of modern techniques and expressive resources.

Extraordinarily difficult to perform are the sonatas and works for the violin alone (**BWV 1001–1006**), works of exceptional beauty among which stands out *Round in B Minor* **BWV 1002**, celebrated especially for its final movement, the *Chaconne*, a dance that has undergone numerous transcriptions for other instruments during the entire modern epoch. But very beautiful are also the six *Suites for Cello Alone* (**BWV 1007–1012**), works that exalt Bach's capacity to write in a polyphonic manner. When listened to, they have the effect of the presence of many voices, even though there is only one instrument. From this pair of compositions, Bach himself drew important transcriptions for the lute alone, while from the joining of other instruments (flute and bass), along with the harpsichord, were born other chamber-music compositions that are today very popular and often performed.

ORCHESTRAL MUSIC

Bach's orchestral production has been almost completely lost; especially that written in Leipzig after 1729, during the many years he was director of the most important *Collegium Musicum* of the city. Of this we have barely a trace. What we do have is a part of his prior production, written mostly for the orchestra of the Court at Köthen between 1717 and 1723, because Bach himself decided to gather in a kind of selective collection some of his best works. In this way was born in about 1720 the autograph of six *Concertos for Many Instruments* that Bach sent as a gift to the Margrave of Brandenburg. For this reason they are known today as *The Brandenburg Concertos* (**BWV 1046–1051**). The manner in which they were written represent a synthesis of the Baroque's characteristic style and show how far ahead Bach proceeded on the road of "gallant" music of the period. In each of the six *Brandenburg Concertos,* the protagonist is a different instrumental ensemble or a different soloist. In Concerto No. 5, which features the harpsichord, Bach wrote a long virtuosic part in which the keyboard instrument seems to play by itself, with the orchestra pausing to listen. This technique anticipated a formula, known as the cadenza, that was typical of the classical concerto from Mozart to Beethoven.

In addition to *The Brandenburg Concertos,* we have Bach's suites for the orchestra, also called overtures, in which the dancing style of French music prevails. But above all, we have numerous concertos for one or more harpsichords (**BWV 1052–1065**) and some very beautiful concertos for the violin (**BWV 1041–1042**). The one in D Minor for two violins, strings, and continuo **BWV 1043** is among the most fascinating, and the compact dialogue between the two instruments—that throw the melodies back and forth between themselves—even anticipates the models of the classical concertos.

THE SPECULATIVE WORKS

Bach has always worked on music according to strict geometric and mathematical criteria, considering order and proportion to be elements of absolute aesthetic value. In his last creative phase, he accented this characteristic to produce works that were ever more abstract and speculative, idealizing the techniques of composing to the point of making completely secondary the "pleasing" effects that were given such great consideration by the styles of the time. The beauty of these works comes primarily from the rigor of their construction, from the refinement of the counterpoint, and from the boldness of the harmonic encounters.

The Canonic Variations, for the organ, *The Musical Offering,* and *The Art of the Fugue* are the three works which exemplify this speculative tendency of Bach's. All three were used as annual submissions to the Society of Musical Sciences founded in Leipzig by Lorenz Christoph Mizler, once a former student of Bach's. But they are all different from each other in concept. *The Canonic Variations* **BWV 769** are, in fact, an extension of the traditional organ improvisational technique of variations on a given theme. *The Musical Offering* **BWV 1079**, which was the result of an improvisation at the harpsichord that Bach executed in 1747 at Potsdam upon a theme suggested by Frederick II, develops, on the other hand, as a repertoire of contrapuntal forms for an orchestral ensemble that is variable, but with an important part dedicated to the flute (the instrument of the king). *The Art of the Fugue* **BWV 1080**, then, seems never to have been performed, but is the object of the most diverse transcriptions and adaptations for different kinds of ensembles. It contains fugues of exceptional complexity and concludes with a chant that, according to tradition, the author dictated on his deathbed, but that is more likely an addition by his son, Carl Philipp Emanuel. Bach, in fact, left *The Art of the Fugue* unfinished: his grandiose musical legacy therefore remains the most enigmatic of all his works.

INDEX